Beginning Big Data with Power BI and Excel 2013

Neil Dunlop

Apress®

Beginning Big Data with Power BI and Excel 2013

ISBN-13 (pbk): 978-1-4842-0530-3

ISBN-13 (electronic): 978-1-4842-0529-7

Managing Director: Welmoed Spahr
Lead Editor: Jonathan Gennick
Development Editor: Douglas Pundick
Technical Reviewer: Kathi Kellenberger
Editorial Board: Steve Anglin, Mark Beckner, Gary Cornell, Louise Corrigan, Jim DeWolf,
    Jonathan Gennick, Robert Hutchinson, Michelle Lowman, James Markham, Susan McDermott,
    Matthew Moodie, Jeffrey Pepper, Douglas Pundick, Ben Renow-Clarke, Gwenan Spearing,
    Matt Wade, Steve Weiss
Coordinating Editor: Jill Balzano
Copy Editor: Michael G. Laraque
Compositor: SPi Global
Indexer: SPi Global
Artist: SPi Global
Cover Designer: Anna Ishchenko

Distributed to the book trade worldwide by Springer Science+Business Media New York, 233 Spring Street, 6th Floor, New York, NY 10013. Phone 1-800-SPRINGER, fax (201) 348-4505, e-mail orders-ny@springer-sbm.com, or visit www.springeronline.com. Apress Media, LLC is a California LLC and the sole member (owner) is Springer Science + Business Media Finance Inc (SSBM Finance Inc). SSBM Finance Inc is a Delaware corporation.

For information on translations, please e-mail rights@apress.com, or visit www.apress.com.

Apress and friends of ED books may be purchased in bulk for academic, corporate, or promotional use. eBook versions and licenses are also available for most titles. For more information, reference our Special Bulk Sales–eBook Licensing web page at www.apress.com/bulk-sales.

Any source code or other supplementary material referenced by the author in this text is available to readers at www.apress.com. For additional information about how to locate and download your book's source code, go to www.apress.com/source-code/.

Contents at a Glance

Contents

About the Author

Neil Dunlop is a professor of business and computer information systems at Berkeley City College, Berkeley, California. He served as chairman of the Business and Computer Information Systems Departments for many years. He has more than 35 years' experience as a computer programmer and software designer and is the author of three books on database management. He is listed in Marquis's *Who's Who in America*. Check out his blog at http://bigdataondesktop.com/.

About the Technical Reviewer

Kathi Kellenberger, known to the Structured Query Language (SQL) community as Aunt Kathi, is an independent SQL Server consultant associated with Linchpin People and an SQL Server MVP. She loves writing about SQL Server and has contributed to a dozen books as an author, coauthor, or technical editor. Kathi enjoys spending free time with family and friends, especially her five grandchildren. When she is not working or involved in a game of hide-and-seek or Candy Land with the kids, you may find her at the local karaoke bar. Kathi blogs at www.auntkathisql.com.

Acknowledgments

I would like to thank everyone at Apress for their help in learning the Apress system and getting me over the hurdles of producing this book. I would also like to thank my colleagues at Berkeley City College for understanding my need for time to write.

Introduction

This book is intended for anyone with a basic knowledge of Excel who wants to analyze and visualize data in order to get results. It focuses on understanding the underlying structure of data, so that the most appropriate tools can be used to analyze it. The early working title of this book was "Big Data for the Masses," implying that these tools make Business Intelligence (BI) more accessible to the average person who wants to leverage his or her Excel skills to analyze large datasets.

As discussed in Chapter 1, big data is more about volume and velocity than inherent complexity. This book works from the premise that many small- to medium-sized organizations can meet most of their data needs with Excel and Power BI. The book demonstrates how to import big data file formats such as JSON, XML, and HDFS and how to filter larger datasets down to thousands or millions of rows instead of billions.

This book starts out by showing how to import various data formats into Excel (Chapter 2) and how to use Pivot Tables to extract summary data from a single table (Chapter 3). Chapter 5 demonstrates how to use Structured Query Language (SQL) in Excel. Chapter 10 offers a brief introduction to statistical analysis in Excel.

This book primarily covers Power BI—Microsoft's self-service BI tool—which includes the following Excel add-ins:

1. *PowerPivot*. This provides the repository for the data (see Chapter 4) and the DAX formula language (see Chapter 7). Chapter 4 provides an example of processing millions of rows in multiple tables.

2. *Power View*. A reporting tool for extracting meaningful reports and creating some of the elements of dashboards (see Chapter 6).

3. *Power Query*. A tool to Extract, Transform, and Load (ETL) data from a wide variety of sources (see Chapter 8).

4. *Power Map*. A visualization tool for mapping data (see Chapter 9).

Chapter 11 demonstrates how to use HDInsight (Microsoft's implementation of Hadoop that runs on its Azure cloud platform) to import big data into Excel.

This book is written for Excel 2013, but most of the examples it includes will work with Excel 2010, if the PowerPivot, Power View, Power Query, and Power Map add-ins are downloaded from Microsoft. Simply search on download and the add-in name to find the download link.

▓ **Disclaimer**   All links and screenshots were current at the time of writing but may have changed since publication. The author has taken all due care in describing the processes that were accurate at the time of writing, but neither the author nor the publisher is liable for incidental or consequential damages arising from the furnishing or performance of any information or procedures.

CHAPTER 1

Big Data

The goal of business today is to unlock intelligence stored in data. We are seeing a confluence of trends leading to an exponential increase in available data, including cheap storage and the availability of sensors to collect data. Also, the Internet of Things, in which objects interact with other objects, will generate vast amounts of data.

Organizations are trying to extract intelligence from unstructured data. They are striving to break down the divisions between silos. Big data and NoSQL tools are being used to analyze this avalanche of data.

Big data has many definitions, but the bottom line involves extracting insights from large amounts of data that might not be obvious, based on smaller data sets. It can be used to determine which products to sell, by analyzing buying habits to predict what products customers want to purchase. This chapter will cover the evolution of data analysis tools from early primitive maps and graphs to the big data tools of today.

Big Data As the Fourth Factor of Production

Traditional economics, based on an industrial economy, teaches that there are three factors of production: land, labor, and capital. The December 27, 2012, issue of the *Financial Times* included an article entitled "Why 'Big Data' is the fourth factor of production," which examines the role of big data in decision making. According to the article "As the prevalence of Big Data grows, executives are becoming increasingly wedded to numerical insight. But the beauty of Big Data is that it allows both intuitive and analytical thinkers to excel. More entrepreneurially minded, creative leaders can find unexpected patterns among disparate data sources (which might appeal to their intuitive nature) and ultimately use the information to alter the course of the business."

Big Data As Natural Resource

IBM's CEO Virginia Rometty has been quoted as saying "Big Data is the world's natural resource for the next century." She also added that data needs to be refined in order to be useful. IBM has moved away from hardware manufacturing and invested $30 billion to enhance its big data capabilities.

Much of IBM's investment in big data has been in the development of Watson—a natural language, question-answering computer. Watson was introduced as a *Jeopardy!* player in 2011, when it won against previous champions. It has the computing power to search 1 million books per second. It can also process colloquial English.

One of the more practical uses of Watson is to work on cancer treatment plans in collaboration with doctors. To do this, Watson received input from 2 million pages of medical journals and 600,000 clinical records. When a doctor inputs a patient's symptoms, Watson can produce a list of recommendations ranked in order of confidence of success.

Data As Middle Manager

An April 30, 2015, article in the *Wall Street Journal* by Christopher Mims entitled "Data Is Now the New Middle Manager" describes how some startup companies are substituting data for middle managers. According to the article "Startups are nimbler than they have ever been, thanks to a fundamentally different management structure, one that pushes decision-making out to the periphery of the organization, to the people actually tasked with carrying out the actual business of the company. What makes this relatively flat hierarchy possible is that front line workers have essentially unlimited access to data that used to be difficult to obtain, or required more senior management to interpret." The article goes on to elaborate that when databases were very expensive and business intelligence software cost millions of dollars, it made sense to limit access to top managers. But that is not the case today. Data scientists are needed to validate the accuracy of the data and how it is presented. Mims concludes "Now that every employee can have tools to monitor progress toward any goal, the old role of middle managers, as people who gather information and make decisions, doesn't fit into many startups."

Early Data Analysis

Data analysis was not always sophisticated. It has evolved over the years from the very primitive to where we are today.

First Time Line

In 1765, the theologian and scientist Joseph Priestley created the first time line charts, in which individual bars were used to compare the life spans of multiple persons, such as in the chart shown in Figure 1-1.

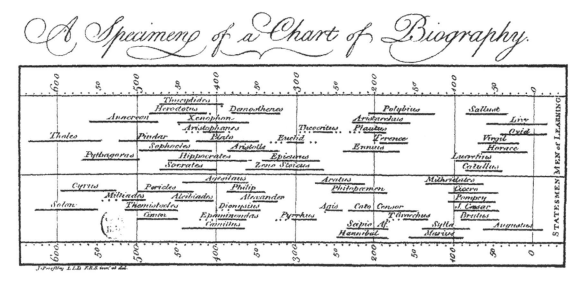

Figure 1-1. *An early time line chart*

First Bar Chart and Time Series

The Scottish engineer William Playfair has been credited with inventing the line, bar, and pie charts. His time-series plots are still presented as models of clarity. Playfair first published *The Commercial and Political Atlas* in London in 1786. It contained 43 time-series plots and one bar chart. It has been described as the first major work to contain statistical graphs. Playfair's *Statistical Breviary*, published in London in 1801, contains what is generally credited as the first pie chart. One of Playfair's time-series charts showing the balance of trade is shown in Figure 1-2.

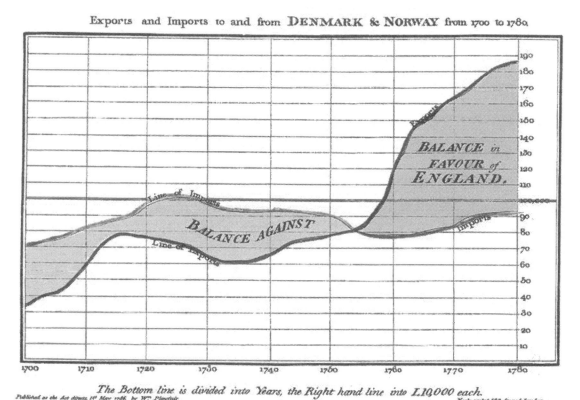

Figure 1-2. *Playfair's balance-of-trade time-series chart*

Cholera Map

In 1854, the physician John Snow mapped the incidence of cholera cases in London to determine the linkage to contaminated water from a single pump, as shown in Figure 1-3. Prior to that analysis, no one knew what caused cholera. This is believed to be the first time that a map was used to analyze how disease is spread.

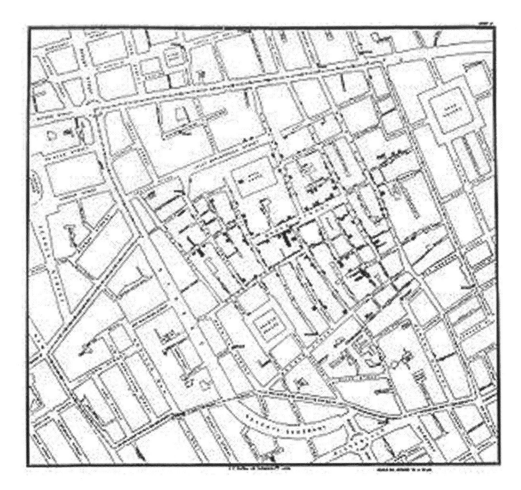

Figure 1-3. *Cholera map*

Modern Data Analytics

The Internet has opened up vast amounts of data. Google and other Internet companies have designed tools to access that data and make it widely available.

Google Flu Trends

In 2009, Google set up a system to track flu outbreaks based on flu-related searches. When the H1N1 crisis struck in 2009, Google's system proved to be a more useful and timely indicator than government statistics with their natural reporting lags (*Big Data* by Viktor Mayer-Schonberger and Kenneth Cukier [Mariner Books, 2013]). However, in 2012, the system overstated the number of flu cases, presumably owing to media attention about the flu. As a result, Google adjusted its algorithm.

Google Earth

The precursor of Google Earth was developed in 2005 by the computer programmer Rebecca Moore, who lived in the Santa Cruz Mountains in California, where a timber company was proposing a logging operation that was sold as fire prevention. Moore used Google Earth to demonstrate that the logging plan would remove forests near homes and schools and threaten drinking water.

Tracking Malaria

A September 10, 2014, article in the *San Francisco Chronicle* reported that a team at the University of California, San Francisco (UCSF) is using Google Earth to track malaria in Africa and to track areas that may be at risk for an outbreak. According to the article, "The UCSF team hopes to zoom in on the factors that make malaria likely to spread: recent rainfall, plentiful vegetation, low elevations, warm temperatures, close proximity to rivers, dense populations." Based on these factors, potential malaria hot spots are identified.

Big Data Cost Savings

According to a July 1, 2014, article in the *Wall Street Journal* entitled "Big Data Chips Away at Cost," Chris Iervolino, research director at the consulting firm Gartner Inc., was quoted as saying "Accountants and finance executives typically focus on line items such as sales and spending, instead of studying the relationships between various sets of numbers. But the companies that have managed to reconcile those information streams have reaped big dividends from big data."

Examples cited in the article include the following:

- Recently, General Motors made a decision to stop selling Chevrolets in Europe based on an analysis of costs compared to projected sales, based on analysis that took a few days rather than many weeks.

- Planet Fitness has been able to analyze the usage of their treadmills based on their location in reference to high-traffic areas of the health club and to rotate them to even out wear on the machines.

Big Data and Governments

Governments are struggling with limited money and people but have an abundance of data. Unfortunately, most governmental organizations don't know how to utilize the data that they have to get resources to the right people at the right time.

The US government has made an attempt to disclose where its money goes through the web site USAspending.gov. The city of Palo Alto, California, in the heart of Silicon Valley, makes its data available through its web site data.cityofpaloalto.org. The goal of the city's use of data is to provide agile, fast government. The web site provides basic data about city operations, including when trees are planted and trimmed.

Predictive Policing

Predictive policing uses data to predict where crime might occur, so that police resources can be allocated with maximum efficiency. The goal is to identify people and locations at increased risk of crime.

A Cost-Saving Success Story

A January 24, 2011, *New Yorker* magazine article described how 30-something physician Jeffrey Brenner mapped crime and medical emergency statistics in Camden, New Jersey, to devise a system that would cut costs, over the objections of the police. He obtained medical billing records from the three main hospitals and crime statistics. He made block-by-block maps of the city, color-coded by the hospital costs of the residents. He found that the two most expensive blocks included a large nursing home and a low-income housing complex. According to the article, "He found that between January 2002 and June of 2008 some nine hundred people in the two buildings accounted for more than four thousand hospital visits and about two hundred million dollars in health-care bills. One patient had three hundred and twenty-four admissions in five years. The most expensive patient cost insurers $3.5 million." He determined that 1% of the patients accounted for 30% of the costs.

Brenner's goal was to most effectively help patients while cutting costs. He tried targeting the sickest patients and providing preventative care and health monitoring, as well as treatment for substance abuse, to minimize emergency room visits and hospitalization. He set up a support system involving a nurse practitioner and a social worker to support the sickest patients. Early results of this approach showed a 56% cost reduction.

Internet of Things or Industrial Internet

The Internet of Things refers to machine to machine (M2M) communication involving networked connectivity between devices, such as home lighting and thermostats. CISCO Systems uses the term *Internet of Everything*.

An article in the July/August 2014 issue of *Fast Company* magazine described how General Electric Corporation (GE) is using the term *Industrial Internet*, which involves putting intelligence into machines to collect and analyze their data in order to predict failure, so that problems can be anticipated and corrected. One example is the GE jet engine. GE plans to use data generated from engines to predict when an engine part requires repairs, so that the problem can be corrected before a failure occurs. GE's assumption is that small gains in productivity and reliability can drive massive economic benefits.

GE is also working on trip-optimizer, an intelligent cruise control for locomotives, which use trains' geographical location, weight, speed, fuel consumption, and terrain to calculate the optimal velocity to minimize fuel consumption.

Cutting Energy Costs at MIT

An article in the September 28, 2014, *Wall Street Journal* entitled "Big Data Cuts Buildings' Energy Use" describes how cheap sensors are allowing collection of real-time data on how energy is being consumed. For example, the Massachusetts Institute of Technology (MIT) has an energy war room in which energy use in campus buildings is monitored. Energy leaks can be detected and corrected.

The Big Data Revolution and Health Care

An April 2013 report from McKinsey & Company entitled "The big-data revolution in US health care: Accelerating value and innovation" describes how a big data revolution is occurring in health care, based on pharmaceutical companies aggregating years of research into medical databases and health care providers digitizing patient records. There is a trend toward evidence-based medicine based on data. Big data algorithms are being used to provide the best evidence.

Health care spending currently accounts for more than 17% of US gross domestic product (GDP). McKinsey estimates that implementation of these big data strategies in health care could reduce health expenses in the United States by 12% to 17%, saving between $300 billion to $450 billion per year.

"Biological research will be important, but it feels like data science will do more for medicine than all the biological sciences combined," according to the venture capitalist Vinod Khosla, speaking at the Stanford University School of Medicine's Big Data in Biomedicine Conference (quoted in the *San Francisco Chronicle*, May 24, 2014). He went on to say that human judgment cannot compete against machine learning systems that derive predictions from millions of data points. He further predicted that technology will replace 80%–90% of doctors' roles in decision making.

The Medicalized Smartphone

A January 10, 2015, *Wall Street Journal* article reported that "the medicalized smartphone is going to upend every aspect of health care." Attachments to smartphones are being developed that can measure blood pressure and even perform electrocardiograms. Wearable wireless sensors can track blood-oxygen and glucose levels, blood pressure, and heart rhythm. Watches will be coming out that can continually capture blood pressure and other vital signs. The result will be much more data and the potential for virtual physician visits to replace physical office visits.

In December 2013, IDC Health Insights released a report entitled "U.S. Connected Health 2014 Top 10 Predictions: The New Care Delivery Model" that predicts a new health care delivery model involving mobile health care apps, telehealth, and social networking that will provide "more efficient and cost-effective ways to provide health care outside the four walls of the traditional healthcare setting." According to the report, these changes will rely on four transformative technologies:

1. Mobile

2. Big data analytics

3. Social

4. Cloud

The report cites the Smartphone Physical project at Johns Hopkins. It uses "a variety of smartphone-based medical devices that can collect quantitative or qualitative data that is clinically relevant for a physical examination such as body weight, blood pressure, heart rate, blood oxygen saturation, visual acuity, optic disc and tympanic membrane images, pulmonary function values, electrocardiogram, heart and lung sounds and ultrasound visualization (such as carotid artery imaging)."

According to the report, "With greater consumer uptake of mobile health, personal health, and fitness modeling, and social technologies, there will be a proliferation of consumer data across diverse data sources that will yield rich information about consumers."

A May 2011 paper by McKinsey & Company entitled "Big data: The next frontier for innovation, competition, and productivity" posits five ways in which using big data can create value, as follows:

1. Big data can unlock significant value by making information transparent and usable in much higher frequency.

2. As organizations create and store more transactional data in digital form, they can collect more accurate and detailed performance information on everything from product inventories to sick days, and therefore boost performance.

3. Big data allows ever-narrower segmentation of customers and, therefore, much more precisely tailored products or services.

4. Sophisticated analytics can substantially improve decision making.

5. Big data can be used to improve the development of the next generation of products and services.

Improving Reliability of Industrial Equipment

General Electric (GE) has made implementing the Industrial Internet a top priority, in order to improve the reliability of industrial equipment such as jet engines. The company now collects 50 million data points each day from 1.4 million pieces of medical equipment and 28,000 jet engines. The goal is to improve the reliability of the equipment. GE has developed Predix, which can be used to analyze data generated by other companies to build and deploy software applications.

Big Data and Agriculture

The goal of precision agriculture is to increase agricultural productivity to generate enough food as the population of the world increases. Data is collected on soil and air quality, elevation, nitrogen in soil, crop maturity, weather forecasts, equipment, and labor costs. The data is used to determine when to plant, irrigate, fertilize, and harvest. This is achieved by installing sensors to measure temperature and the humidity of soil. Pictures are taken of fields that show crop maturity. Predictive weather modeling is used to plan when to irrigate and harvest. The goal is to increase crop yields, decrease costs, save time, and use less water.

Cheap Storage

In the early 1940s, before physical computers came into general use, *computer* was a job title. The first wave of computing was about speeding up calculations. In 1946, the Electrical Numerical Integrator and Computer (ENIAC)—the first general purpose electronic computer—was installed at the University of Pennsylvania. The ENIAC, which occupied an entire room, weighed 30 tons, and used more than 18,000 vacuum tubes, had been designed to calculate artillery trajectories. However, World War II was over by 1946, so the computer was then used for peaceful applications.

Personal Computers and the Cost of Storage

Personal computers came into existence in the 1970s with Intel chips and floppy drives for storage and were used primarily by hobbyists. In August 1981, the IBM PC was released with 5¼-inch floppy drives that stored 360 kilobytes of data. The fact that IBM, the largest computer company in the world, released a personal computer was a signal to other companies that the personal computer was a serious tool for offices. In 1983, IBM released the IBM-XT, which had a 10 megabyte hard drive that cost hundreds of dollars. Today, a terabyte hard drive can be purchased for less than $100. Multiple gigabyte flash drives can be purchased for under $10.

Review of File Sizes

Over the history of the personal computer, we have gone from kilobytes to megabytes and gigabytes and now terabytes and beyond, as storage needs have grown exponentially. Early personal computers had 640 kilobytes of RAM. Bill Gates, cofounder of Microsoft Corporation, reportedly said that no one would ever need more than 640 kilobytes. Versions of Microsoft's operating system MS-DOS released during the 1980s could only address 640 kilobytes of RAM. One of the selling points of Windows was that it could address more than 640 kilobytes. Table 1-1 shows how data is measured.

Table 1-1. *Measurement of Storage Capacity*

Unit	Power of 2	Approximate Number
Kilobytes	$2^{\wedge}10$	Thousands
Megabytes	$2^{\wedge}20$	Millions
Gigabytes	$2^{\wedge}30$	Billions
Terabytes	$2^{\wedge}40$	Trillions
Petabytes	$2^{\wedge}50$	Quadrillions
Exabytes	$2^{\wedge}60$	Sextillions
Zettabytes	$2^{\wedge}70$	Septillions

Data Keeps Expanding

The New York Stock Exchange generates 4 to 5 terabytes of data every day. IDC estimates that the digital universe was 4.4 petabytes in 2013 and is forecasting a tenfold increase by 2920, to 44 zettabytes.

We are also dealing with exponential growth in Internet connections. According to CISCO Systems, the 15 billion worldwide network connections today are expected to grow to 50 billion by 2020.

Relational Databases

As computers became more and more widely available, more data was stored, and software was needed to organize that data. Relational database management systems (RDBMS) are based on the relational model developed by E. F. Codd at IBM in the early 1970s. Even though the early work was done at IBM, the first commercial RDBMS were released by Oracle in 1979.

A relational database organizes data into tables of rows and columns, with a unique key for each row, called the primary key. A database is a collection of tables. Each entity in a database has its own table, with the rows representing instances of that entity. The columns store values for the attributes or fields.

Relational algebra, first described by Codd at IBM, provides a theoretical foundation for modeling the data stored in relational databases and defining queries. Relational databases support selection, projection, and joins. *Selection* means selecting specified rows of a table based on a condition. *Projection* entails selecting certain specified columns or attributes. *Joins* means joining two or more tables, based on a condition.

As discussed in Chapter 5, Structured Query Language (SQL) was first developed by IBM in the early 1970s. It was used to manipulate and retrieve data from early IBM relational database management systems (RDBMS). It was later implemented in other relational database management systems by Oracle and later Microsoft.

Normalization

Normalization is the process of organizing data in a database with the following objectives:

1. To avoid repeating fields, except for key fields, which link tables

2. To avoid multiple dependencies, which means avoiding fields that depend on anything other than the primary key

There are several normal forms, the most common being the Third Normal Form (3NF), which is based on eliminating transitive dependencies, meaning eliminating fields not dependent on the primary key. In other words, data is in the 3NF when each field depends on the primary key, the whole primary key, and nothing but the primary key.

Figure 1-4, which is the same as Figure 4-11, shows relationships among multiple tables. The lines with arrows indicate relationships between tables. There are three primary types of relationships.

1. One to one (1-1) means that there is a one-to-one correspondence between fields. Generally, fields with a one-to-one correspondence would be in the same table.

2. One to many means that for each record in one table, there are many records in the corresponding table. The many is indicated by an arrow at the end of the line. Many means zero to n. For example, as shown in Figure 1-4, for each product code in the products table, there could be many instances of Product ID in the order details table, but each Product ID is associated with only one product code in the products table.

3. Many to many means a relationship from many of one entity to many of another entity. For example, authors and books: Each author can have many books, and each book can have many authors. Many means zero to n.

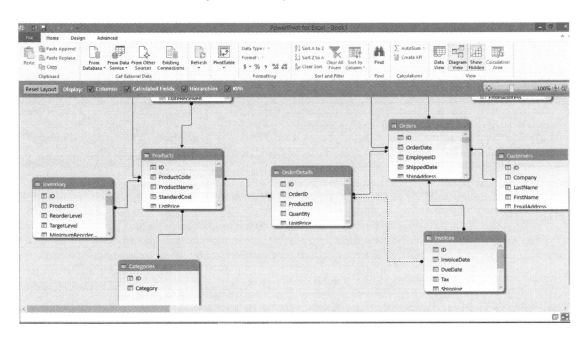

Figure 1-4. *Showing relations among tables*

Database Software for Personal Computers

In the 1980s, database programs were developed for personal computers, as they became more widely used. dBASE II, one of the first relational programmable database systems for personal computers, was developed by Wayne Ratliff at the Jet Propulsion Lab (JPL) in Pasadena, California. In the early 1980s, he partnered with George Tate to form the Ashton-Tate company to market dBASE II, which became very successful. In the mid-1980s, dBASE III was released with enhanced features.

dBASE programs were interpreted, meaning that they ran more slowly than a compiled program, where all the instructions are translated to machine language at once. Clipper was released in 1985 as a compiled version of dBASE and became very popular. A few years later, FoxBase, which later became FoxPro, was released with additional enhanced features.

The Birth of Big Data and NoSQL

The Internet was popularized during the 1990s, owing in part to the World Wide Web, which made it easier to use. Competing search engines allowed users to easily find data. Google was founded in 1996 and revolutionized search. As more data became available, the limitations of relational databases, which tried to fit everything into rectangular tables, became clear.

In 1998, Carlo Strozzi used the term *NoSQL*. He reportedly later regretted using that term and thought that *NoRel*, or non-relational, would have been a better term.

Hadoop Distributed File System (HDFS)

Much of the technology of big data came out of the search engine companies. Hadoop grew out of Apple Nutch, an open source web search engine that was started in 2002. It included a web crawler and search engine, but it couldn't scale to handle billions of web pages.

A paper was published in 2003 that described the architecture of Google's Distributed File System (GFS), which was being used by Google to store the large files generated by web crawling and indexing. In 2004, an open source version was released as the Nutch Distributed File System (NDFS).

In 2004, Google published a paper about MapReduce. By 2005, MapReduce had been incorporated into Nutch. MapReduce is a batch query process with the ability to run ad hoc queries against a large dataset. It unlocks data that was previously archived. Running queries can take several minutes or longer.

In February 2006, Hadoop was set up as an independent subproject. Building on his prior work with Mike Cafarella, Doug Cutting went to work for Yahoo!, which provided the resources to turn Hadoop into a system that could be a useful tool for the Web. By 2008, Yahoo! based its search index on a Hadoop cluster. Hadoop was titled based on the name that Doug Cutting's child gave a yellow stuffed elephant. Hadoop provides a reliable, scalable platform for storage and analysis running on cheap commodity hardware. Hadoop is open source.

Big Data

There is no single definition of big data, but there is currently a lot of hype surrounding it, so the meaning can be diluted. It is generally accepted to mean large volumes of data with an irregular structure involving hundreds of terabytes of data into petabytes and higher. It can include data from financial transactions, sensors, web logs, and social media. A more operational definition is that organizations have to use big data when their data processing needs get too big for traditional relational databases.

Big data is based on the feedback economy where the Internet of Things places sensors on more and more equipment. More and more data is being generated as medical records are digitized, more stores have loyalty cards to track consumer purchases, and people are wearing health-tracking devices. Generally, big data is more about looking at behavior, rather than monitoring transactions, which is the domain of traditional relational databases. As the cost of storage is dropping, companies track more and more data to look for patterns and build predictive models.

The Three V's

One way of characterizing big data is through the three V's:

1. *Volume*: How much data is involved?

2. *Velocity*: How fast is it generated?

3. *Variety*: Does it have irregular structure and format?

Two other V's that are sometimes used are

1. *Variability*: Does it involve a variety of different formats with different interpretations?

2. *Veracity*: How accurate is the data?

The Data Life Cycle

The data life cycle involves collecting and analyzing data to build predictive models, following these steps:

1. Collect the data.

2. Store the data.

3. Query the data to identify patterns and make sense of it.

4. Use visualization tools to find the business value.

5. Predict future consumer behavior based on the data.

Apache Hadoop

Hadoop is an open source software framework written in Java for distributed storage and processing of very large datasets stored on commodity servers. It has built-in redundancy to handle hardware failures. Hadoop is based on two main technologies: MapReduce and the Hadoop Distributed File System (HDFS). Hadoop was created by Doug Cutting and Mike Cafarella in 2005.

MapReduce Algorithm

MapReduce was developed at Google and released through a 2004 paper describing how to use parallel processing to deal with large amounts of data. It was later released into the public domain. It involves a two-step batch process.

1. First, the data is partitioned and sent to mappers, which generate key value pairs.

2. The key value pairs are then collated, so that the values for each key are together, and then the reducer processes the key value pairs to calculate one value per key.

One example that is often cited is a word count. It involves scanning through a manuscript and counting the instances of each word. In this example, each word is a key, and the number of times each word is used is the value.

Hadoop Distributed File System (HDFS)

HDFS is a distributed file system that runs on commodity servers. It is based on the Google File System (GFS). It splits files into blocks and distributes them among the nodes of the cluster. Data is replicated so that if one server goes down, no data is lost. The data is immutable, meaning that tables cannot be edited; it can only be written to once, like CD-R, which is based on write once read many. New data can be appended to an existing file, or the old file can be deleted and the new data written to a new file. HDFS is very expandable, by adding more servers to handle more data.

Some implementations of HDFS are append only, meaning that underlying tables cannot be edited. Instead, writes are logged, and then the file is re-created.

Commercial Implementations of Hadoop

Hadoop is an open source Apache project, but several companies have developed their own commercial implementations. Hortonworks, which was founded by Doug Cutting and other former Yahoo! employees, is one of those companies that offers a commercial implementation. Other such companies include Cloudera and MapR. Another Hadoop implementation is Microsoft's HD Insight, which runs on the Azure cloud platform. An example in Chapter 11 shows how to import an HD Insight database into Power Query.

CAP Theorem

An academic way to look at NoSQL databases includes the CAP Theorem. CAP is an acronym for Consistency, Availability, and Partition Tolerance. According to this theorem, any database can only have two of those attributes. Relational databases have consistency and partition tolerance. Large relational databases are weak on availability, because they have low latency when they are large. NoSQL databases offer availability and partition tolerance but are weak on consistency, because of a lack of fixed structure.

NoSQL

As discussed elsewhere in this book, NoSQL is a misnomer. It does not mean "no SQL." A better term for this type of database might be *non-relational*. NoSQL is designed to access data that has no relational structure, with little or no schema. Early versions of NoSQL required a programmer to write a custom program to retrieve that data. More and more implementations of NoSQL databases today implement some form of SQL for retrieval of data. A May 29, 2015, article on Data Informed by Timothy Stephan entitled "What NoSQL Needs Most Is SQL" (http://data-informed.com/what-nosql-needs-most-is-sql/) makes the case for more SQL access to NoSQL databases.

NoSQL is appropriate for "web scale" data, which is based on high volumes with millions of concurrent users.

Characteristics of NoSQL Data

NoSQL databases are used to access non-relational data that doesn't fit into relational tables. Generally, relational databases are used for mission-critical transactional data. NoSQL databases are typically used for analyzing non-mission-critical data, such as log files.

Implementations of NoSQL

There are several categories of NoSQL databases:

- *Key-Value Stores*: This type of database stores data in rows, but the schema may differ from row to row. Some examples of this type of NoSQL database are Couchbase, Redis, and Riak.

- *Document Stores*: This type of database works with documents that are JSON objects. Each document has properties and values. Some examples are CouchDB, Cloudant, and MongoDB.

- *Wide Column Stores*: This type of database has column families that consist of individual column of key-value pairs. Some example of this type of database are HBase and Cassandra.

- *Graph*: Graph databases are good for social network applications. They have nodes that are like rows in a table. Neo4j is an example of this type of database.

One product that allows accessing data from Hadoop is Hive, which provides an SQL-like language called HiveQL for querying Hadoop. Another product is Pig, which uses Pig Latin for querying. The saying is that 10 lines of Pig Latin do the work of 200 lines of Java.

Spark

Another technology that is receiving a lot of attention is Apache Spark—an open source cluster computing framework originally developed at UC Berkeley in 2009. It uses an in-memory technology that purportedly provides performance up to 100 times faster than Hadoop. It offers Spark SQL for querying. IBM recently announced that it will devote significant resources to the development of Spark.

Microsoft Self-Service BI

Most of these big data and NoSQL technologies came out of search engine and online retailers that process vast amounts of data. For the smaller to medium-size organizations that are processing thousands or millions of rows of data, this book shows how to tap into Microsoft's Power BI running on top of Excel.

Much has been written about the maximum number of rows that can be loaded into PowerPivot. The following link to a blog post at Microsoft Trends documents loading 122 million records: `www.microsofttrends.com/2014/02/09/how-much-data-can-powerpivot-really-manage-how-about-122-million-records`.

Summary

This chapter provides a brief history of the evolution of data analysis, culminating with the big data tools of today. It covers the evolution of data structures, from relational databases to the less structured data that NoSQL addresses.

CHAPTER 2

■ ■ ■

Excel As Database and Data Aggregator

Spreadsheets have a long history of making data accessible to ordinary people. This chapter chronicles the evolution of Excel from spreadsheet to powerful database. It then shows how to import data from a variety of sources. Subsequent chapters will demonstrate how Excel with Power BI is now a powerful Business Intelligence tool.

From Spreadsheet to Database

The first spreadsheet program, VisiCalc (a contraction of *visible calculator*), was released in 1979 for the Apple II computer. It was the first "killer app." A saying at the time was that "VisiCalc sold more Apples than Apple." VisiCalc was developed by Dan Bricklin and Bob Franken. Bricklin was attending Harvard Business School and came up with the idea for the program after seeing a professor manually write out a financial model. Whenever the professor wanted to make a change, he had to erase the old data and rewrite the new data. Bricklin realized that this process could be automated, using an electronic spreadsheet running on a personal computer.

In those days, most accounting data was trapped in mainframe programs that required a programmer to modify or access. For this reason, programmers were called the "high priests" of computing, meaning that end users had little control over how programs worked. VisiCalc was very easy to use for a program of that time. It was also very primitive, compared to the spreadsheets of today. For example, all columns had to be the same width in the early versions of VisiCalc.

Success breeds competition. VisiCalc did not run on CP/M computers, which were the business computers of the day. CP/M, an acronym originally for *Control Program/Monitor*, but that later came to mean "Control Program for Microcomputers," was an operating system used in the late 1970s and early 1980s. In 1980, Sorcim came out with SuperCalc as the spreadsheet for CP/M computers. Microsoft released Multiplan in 1982. All of the spreadsheets of the day were menu-driven.

When the IBM PC was released in August 1981, it was a signal to other large companies that the personal computer was a serious tool for big business. VisiCalc was ported to run on the IBM PC but did not take into account the enhanced hardware capabilities of the new computer.

Seeing an opportunity, entrepreneur Mitch Kapor, a friend of the developers of VisiCalc, founded Lotus Development to write a spreadsheet specifically for the IBM PC. He called his spreadsheet program Lotus 1-2-3. The name 1-2-3 indicated that it took the original spreadsheet functionality and added the ability to create graphic charts and perform limited database functionality such as simple sorts.

Lotus 1-2-3 was the first software program to be promoted through television advertising. Lotus 1-2-3 became popular hand-in-hand with the IBM PC, and it was the leading spreadsheet through the early 1990s.

Microsoft Excel was the first spreadsheet using the graphical user interface that was popularized by the Apple Macintosh. Excel was released in 1987 for the Macintosh. It was later ported to Windows. In the early 1990s, as Windows became popular, Microsoft packaged Word and Excel together into Microsoft Office and priced it aggressively. As a result, Excel displaced Lotus 1-2-3 as the leading spreadsheet. Today, Excel is the most widely used spreadsheet program in the world.

More and more analysis features, such as Pivot Tables, were gradually introduced into Excel, and the maximum number of rows that could be processed was increased. Using VLOOKUP, it was possible to create simple relations between tables. For Excel 2010, Microsoft introduced PowerPivot as a separate download, which allowed building a data model based on multiple tables. PowerPivot ships with Excel 2013. Chapter 4 will discuss how to build data models using PowerPivot.

Interpreting File Extensions

The file extension indicates the type of data that is stored in a file. This chapter will show how to import a variety of formats into Excel's native .xlsx format, which is required to use the advanced features of Power BI discussed in later chapters. This chapter will deal with files with the following extensions:

> .xls: Excel workbook prior to Excel 2007

> .xlsx: Excel workbook Excel 2007 and later; the second x was added to indicate that the data is stored in XML format

> .xlsm: Excel workbook with macros

> .xltm: Excel workbook template

> .txt: a file containing text

> .xml: a text file in XML format

Using Excel As a Database

By default, Excel works with tables consisting of rows and columns. Each row is a record that includes all the attributes of a single item. Each column is a field or attribute.

A table should show the field names in the first row and have whitespace around it—a blank column on each side and a blank row above and below, unless the first row is row 1 or the first column is A. Click anywhere inside the table and press Ctrl+T to define it as a table, as shown in Figure 2-1. Notice the headers with arrows at the top of each column. Clicking the arrow brings up a menu offering sorting and filtering options.

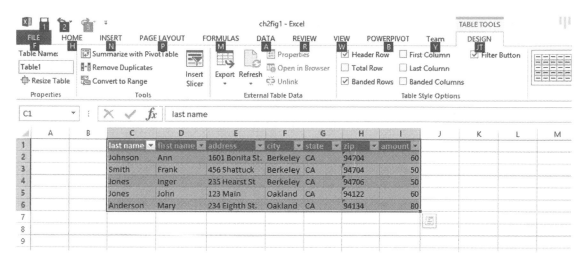

Figure 2-1. *An Excel table*

Note that, with the current version of Excel, if you sort on one field, it is smart enough to bring along the related fields (as long as there are no blank columns in the range), as shown in Figure 2-2, where a sort is done by last name. To sort by first and last name, sort on first name first and then last name.

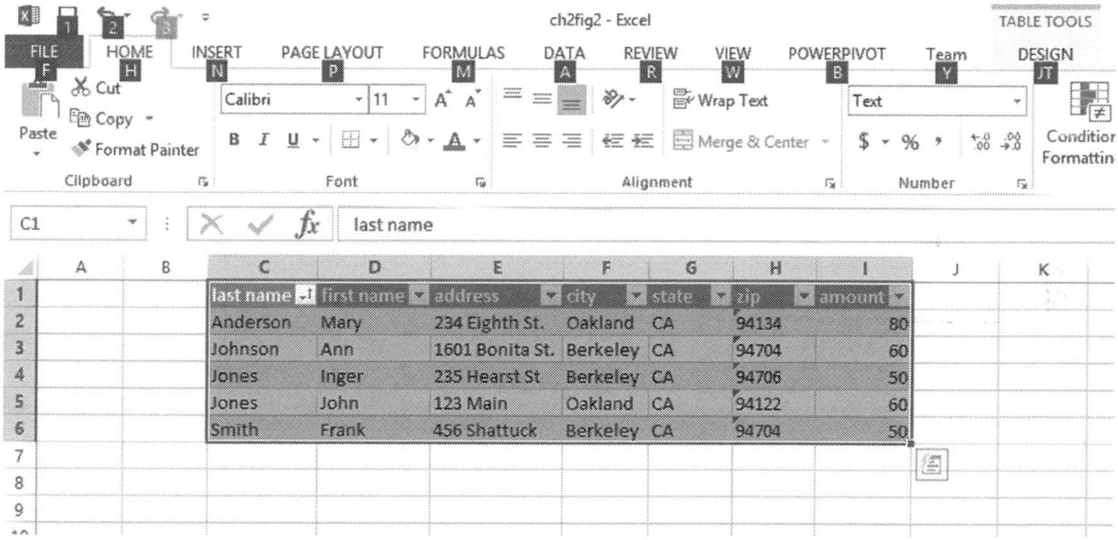

Figure 2-2. *Excel Table sorted by first and last name*

Importing from Other Formats

Excel can be used to import data from a variety of sources, including data stored in text files, data in tables on a web site, data in XML files, and data in JSON format. This chapter will show you how to import some of the more common formats. Chapter 4 will cover how to link multiple tables using Power BI.

Opening Text Files in Excel

Excel can open text files in comma-delimited, tab-delimited, fixed-length-field, and XML formats, as well as in the file formats shown in Figure 2-3. When files in any of these formats are opened in Excel, they are automatically converted to a spreadsheet.

Figure 2-3. *File formats that can be imported into Excel*

When importing files, it is best to work with a copy of the file, so that the original file remains unchanged in case the file is corrupted when it is imported.

Figure 2-4 shows a comma-delimited file in Notepad. Note that the first row consists of the field names. All fields are separated by commas. Excel knows how to read this type of file into a spreadsheet. If a text file in this format is opened with Excel, it will appear as a spreadsheet, as shown in Figure 2-1.

Figure 2-4. *Comma-separated values format*

Importing Data from XML

Extensible Markup Language (XML) is a popular format for storing data. As in HTML, it uses paired tags to define each element. Figure 2-5 shows the data we have been working with in XML format. The first line is the declaration that specifies the version of XML, UTF encoding, and other information. Note the donors root tag that surrounds all of the other tags.

```
contribuxmlrev - Notepad
File  Edit  Format  View  Help
<?xml version="1.0" encoding="UTF-8" standalone="no" ?>
<donors>
        <donor>
            <lname>Johnson</lname>
            <fname>Ann</fname>
            <straddr>1601 Bonita St</straddr>
            <city>Berkeley</city>
            <state>CA</state>
            <zip>94704</zip>
            <amount>60.0</amount>
        </donor>
        <donor >
            <lname>Smith</lname>
            <fname>Frank</fname>
            <straddr>456 Shattuck</straddr>
            <city>Berkeley</city>
            <state>CA</state>
            <zip>94704</zip>
            <amount>50.0</amount>
        </donor>
        <donor>
            <lname>Jones</lname>
            <fname>Inger</fname>
            <straddr>235 Hearst</straddr>
            <city>Berkeley</city>
            <state>CA</state>
            <zip>94706</zip>
            <amount>50.0</amount>
        </donor>
        <donor>
            <lname>Jones</lname>
            <fname>John</fname>
            <straddr>123 Main</straddr>
            <city>Oakland</city>
            <state>CA</state>
            <zip>94122</zip>
            <amount>60.0</amount>
        </donor>
        <donor>
            <lname>Anderson</lname>
            <fname>Mary</fname>
            <straddr>234 Eighth St.</straddr>
            <city>Oakland</city>
            <state>CA</state>
            <zip>94134</zip>
            <amount>80.0</amount>
        </donor>
</donors>
```

Figure 2-5. *XML format*

The data is self-descriptive. Each row or record in this example is surrounded by a donor tag. The field names are repeated twice for each field in the opening and closing tags. This file would be saved as a text file with an .xml extension.

An XML file can be opened directly by Excel. On the first pop-up after it opens, select "As an XML table." Then, on the next pop-up, click yes for "Excel will create the schema."

As shown in Figure 2-6, XML files can be displayed in a web browser such as Internet Explorer. Note the small plus and minus signs to the left of the donor tab. Click minus to hide the details in each record. Click plus to show the details.

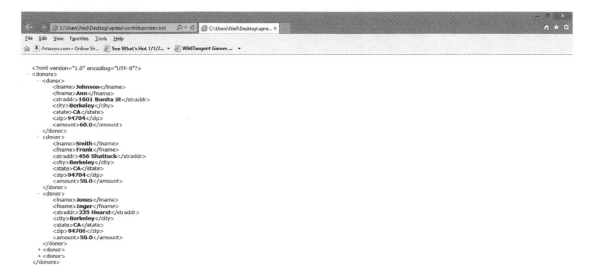

Figure 2-6. *XML file displayed in a web browser*

Importing XML with Attributes

As does HTML, XML can have attributes. Figure 2-7 shows an example of adding a gender attribute as part of the donor tag

```
<donor gender = "female">
...
</donor>
```

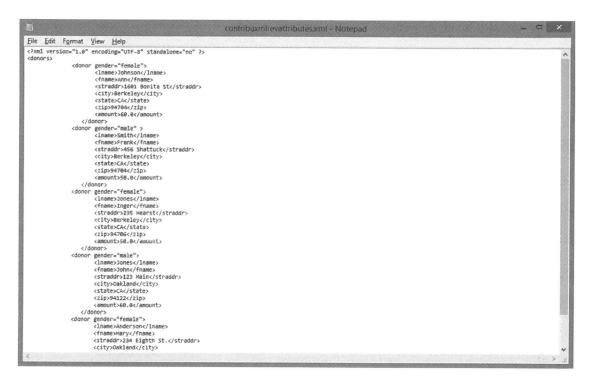

Figure 2-7. *XML with attributes*

There are two schools of thought about using attributes. Some people believe that attributes should be avoided and that all values should be presented in paired tags. However, XML with attributes may be encountered. Excel can interpret either format. Figure 2-8 shows the Excel spreadsheet that would be displayed by opening the XML file shown in Figure 2-7.

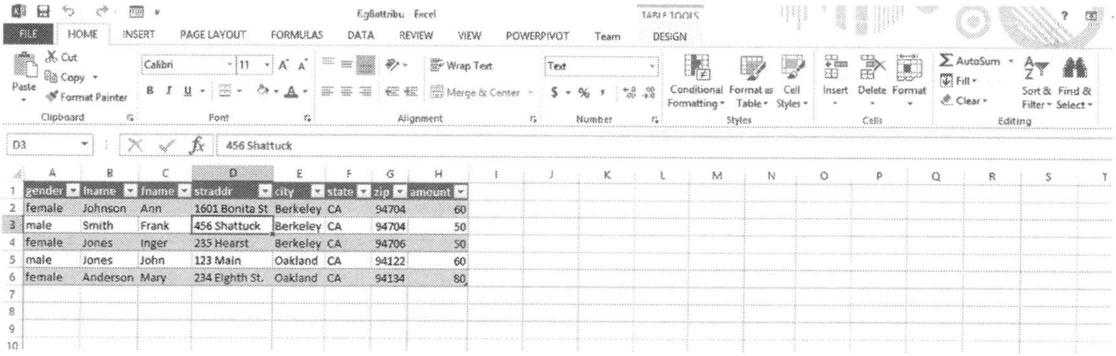

Figure 2-8. *XML with attributes imported into Excel*

Importing JSON Format

Much NoSQL data is stored in JavaScript Object Notation (JSON) format. Unfortunately, Excel does not read JSON files directly, so it is necessary to use an intermediate format to import them into Excel. Figure 2-9 shows our sample file in JSON format. Note the name-value pairs in which each field name is repeated every time there is an instance of that field.

Figure 2-9. *JSON format*

Because Excel cannot read JSON files directly, you would have to convert this JSON-formatted data into a format such as XML that Excel can read. A number of free converters are available on the Web, such as the one at http://bit.ly/1s20i6L.

The interface for the converter is shown in Figure 2-10. (Remember to work with a copy of the file, so that the original will not be corrupted.) The JSON file can be pasted into the JSON window and then converted to XML by clicking the arrow. The result is an XML file having the same name and that you can open directly from Excel.

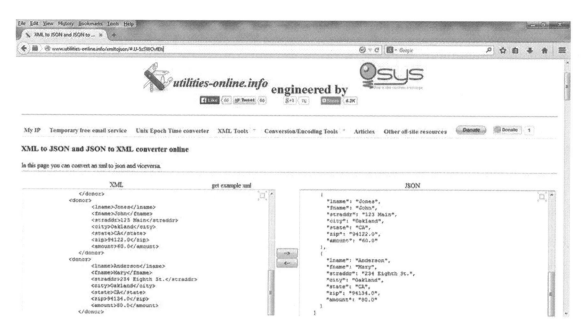

Figure 2-10. *XML and JSON*

Using the Data Tab to Import Data

So far, we have been importing data from text files directly into Excel to create a new spreadsheet. The options on the Data tab can be used to import data from a variety of formats, as part of an existing spreadsheet.

Importing Data from Tables on a Web Site

As an example, let's look at importing data from a table on a web site.

To import data from a table on a web site, do the following:

1. Click the Data tab to display the Data ribbon.

2. Click From Web.

3. A browser window will appear. Type in the address of the web site you want to access. We will access a Bureau of Labor Statistics example of employment based on educational attainment. For this example, we will use http://www.bls.gov/emp/ep_table_education_summary.htm.

4. As shown in Figure 2-11, a black arrow in a small yellow box will appear next to each table. Click the black arrow in the small yellow box at the upper left-hand corner of the table, and it will change to a check mark in a green box. Click Import. The Import Data dialog will appear as shown in Figure 2-12.

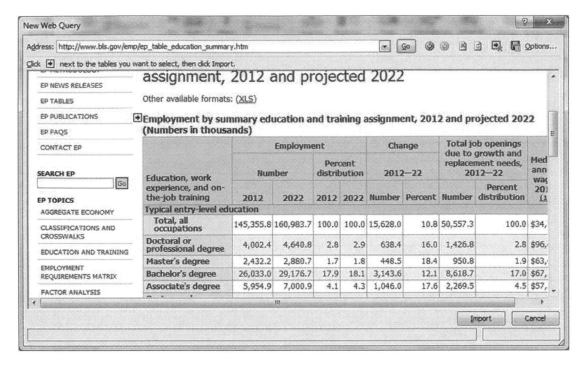

Figure 2-11. *Importing data from the Web*

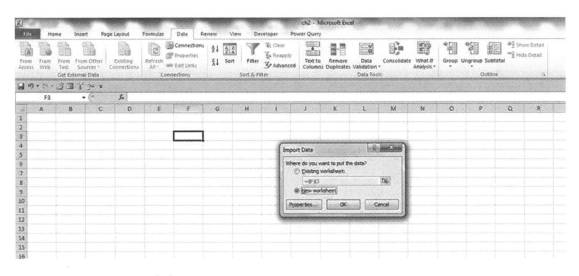

Figure 2-12. *Import Data dialog*

5. Select new Worksheet and then OK. The table will be imported, as shown in
    Figure 2-13. Some formatting may be required in Excel to get the table to be
    precisely as you want it to be for further analysis.

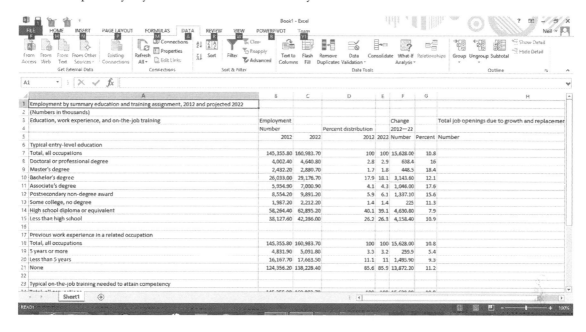

Figure 2-13. *Data from the Web imported into Excel*

Data Wrangling and Data Scrubbing

Imported data is rarely in the form in which it is needed. Data can be problematic for the following reasons:

- It is incomplete.

- It is inconsistent.

- It is in the wrong format.

Data wrangling involves converting raw data into a usable format. *Data scrubbing* means correcting errors and inconsistencies. Excel provides tools to scrub and format data.

Correcting Capitalization

One of the functions that Excel provides to correct capitalization is the Proper() function. It capitalizes the first letter of each word and lowercases the rest. Figure 2-14 shows some text before and after executing the function. To use the Proper() function, as shown in Figure 2-14, perform the following steps:

1. In a new column, type "=Proper(."

2. Click the first cell that you want to apply it to and then type the closing
    parentheses ()). Then press Enter.

3. Click the cell in which you just entered the formula and then drag the fill handle in the lower right corner of the cell, to copy the formula down the column.

4. Convert the content of the cells from formulas to values. For a small number of cells, do that by selecting each cell, pressing F2 to edit, then pressing F9 to convert to values, and then pressing Enter.

5. For a larger number of cells, select the column, right-click, and select copy. Then select the top cell in the range to be copied to, press Ctrl+Alt+V, to open the Paste Special Box, select Values, and click OK.

6. Then you can delete the original column by right-clicking anywhere in the column and selecting Delete ➤ Entire Column.

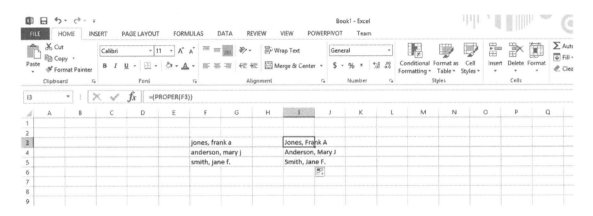

Figure 2-14. *Use of the Proper( ) function*

Splitting Delimited Fields

In some cases, first and last names are included in the same field and are separated by commas. These and similar fields can be split using the Text to Columns option on the Data tab.

1. Highlight the range of cells that you want to convert.

2. Click Text to Columns on the Data tab. In the pop-up window, select Delimited, as shown in Figure 2-15. Then click Next.

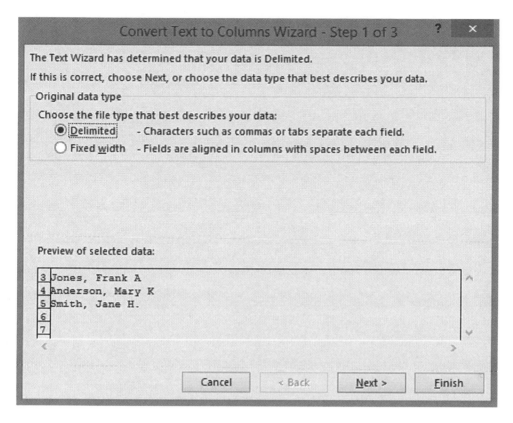

Figure 2-15. *Convert Text to Columns Dialog*

3. On the next pop-up window, shown in Figure 2-16, select Comma and Space as the delimiters and review the preview. If the preview looks right, click Next. The reason for including the space as a delimiter is to accommodate middle initials, which are, in this example, separated from their respective first names by a space.

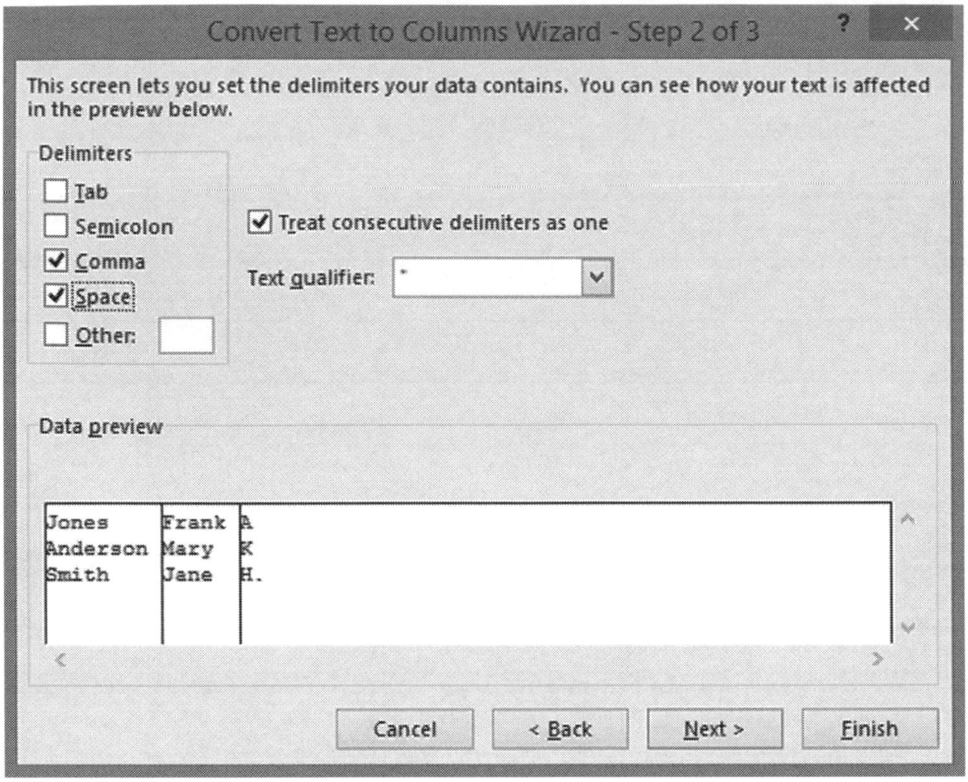

Figure 2-16. Data preview of Text to Columns

4. In the next pop-up window, select each column in the Data Preview window and click Text as the format, as shown in Figure 2-17. Enter the destination where you want the results to appear, then click Finish.

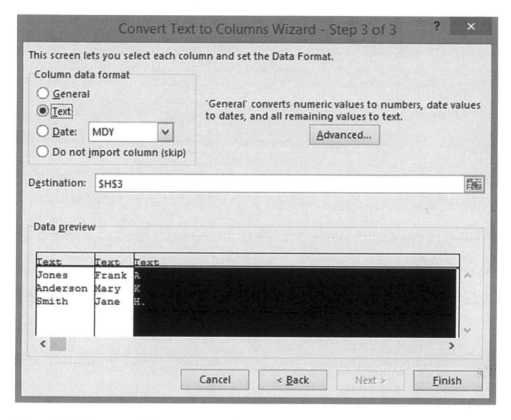

Figure 2-17. *Last step of Convert Text to Columns*

Splitting Complex, Delimited Fields

More complex cases involving multiple data elements in a single field can often be solved through using Excel's built-in functions. Some of the functions that are available for string manipulation are shown in Table 2-1.

Table 2-1. *Available Functions for String Manipulation*

Function	Description
LEN(text)	Returns the number of characters in the text string
LEFT(text,num_chars)	Returns the leftmost number of characters specified by num_chars
RIGHT(text,num_chars)	Returns the rightmost number of characters specified by num_chars
MID(text,start,num_chars)	Returns the number of characters specified by num_chars, starting from the position specified by start
SEARCH(find_text, within_text,start_num)	Returns the position at which the specified find_text starts in within_text when reading from left to right. Not case sensitive. start_num specifies the occurrence of the text that you want. The default is 1.

(*continued*)

Table 2-1. (*continued*)

Function	Description
TRIM(text)	Removes all leading and trailing spaces from a text string, except single spaces between words
CLEAN(text)	Removes all non-printable characters from a text string
LOWER(text)	Returns string with all characters converted to lower case
UPPER(text)	Returns string with all characters converted to upper case
PROPER(text)	Returns string with first letter of each word in upper case

Functions can be nested. For example, we could extract the last name by using the following formula:

```
=LEFT(F7,SEARCH(",",F7)-1)
```

This function would extract the leftmost characters up to the position of the comma. To extract the first name and middle initial, use the following:

```
=RIGHT(F7,SEARCH(", ",F7)+1)
```

Removing Duplicates

It is not unusual for imported data to include duplicate records. Duplicate records can be removed by using the Remove Duplicates option on the Data tab.

It is always a good idea to work with a copy of the original files, to prevent valid data from being deleted. To delete duplicates, simply highlight the columns that contain duplicate values and click Remove Duplicates, as shown in Figure 2-18. Confirm the columns that contain duplicates and click OK. Only the rows in which all the values are the same will be removed.

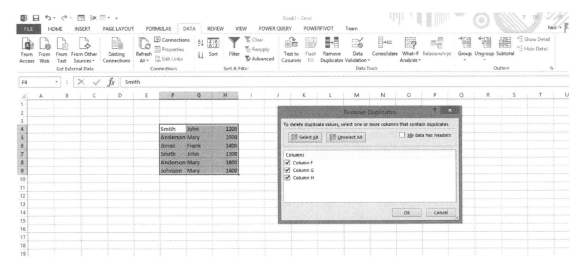

Figure 2-18. *Removing duplicates*

Input Validation

Excel provides tools to check for valid input. If data is not valid, the result can be Garbage In, Garbage Out (GIGO). Excel provides data validation tools that are usually associated with data entry; however, they can be used to flag cells from data that has already been entered. In the example shown in Figure 2-19, the valid range for sales figures is 0 to $20,000, as defined through the Data Validation option on the Data tab.

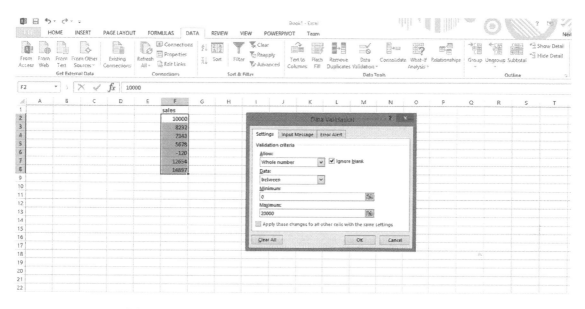

Figure 2-19. *Data Validation dialog*

Any values outside of the range can be highlighted by selecting the Circle Invalid Data option under Data Validation on the Data tab. The result is shown in Figure 2-20.

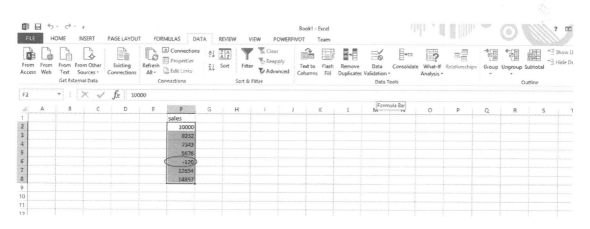

Figure 2-20. *Invalid data flagged with red circle*

Working with Data Forms

One of the hidden and less documented features in Excel is the Data Forms feature. Sometimes it is easier to read data in which each record is displayed as a form rather than just in tabular format. By default, there is no Data Forms icon on the toolbars. Data Forms can be accessed by clicking a cell in a table with row headings and pressing Alt+D and then O (as in Oscar). Data Forms can also be added to the Quick Access Toolbar. This can be done via the following steps:

1. Click the down arrow at the rightmost end of the Quick Access Toolbar (located at the top-left section of the screen) and click More Commands, as shown in Figure 2-21.

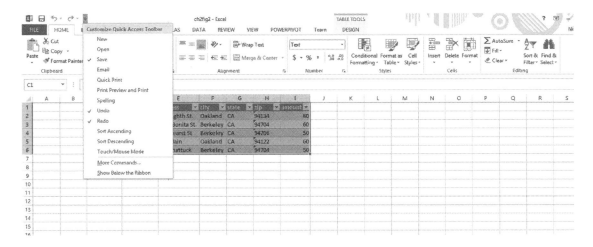

Figure 2-21. *Customize Quick Access Toolbar menu*

2. After clicking More Commands, select "Commands Not in the Ribbon," at the top of the screen. The screen shown in Figure 2-22 will appear. Find and select the icon for forms and press the Add ➤ button in the middle to put it on the Quick Access Toolbar.

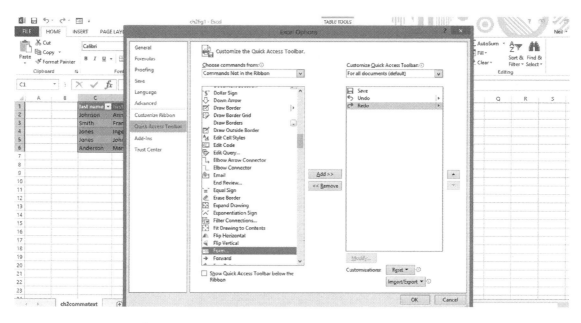

Figure 2-22. *Customize the Quick Access Toolbar menu*

3. To use data forms, click the row that contains the data to be viewed in the form. Then click the Form icon in the Quick Access Toolbar to see the display shown in Figure 2-23. Fields can be edited in the data form. Click the Find Next and Find Previous buttons to move through the records.

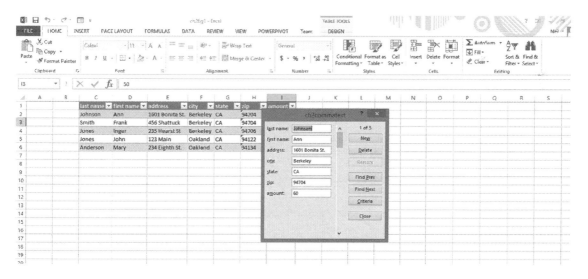

Figure 2-23. *Using a data form*

Selecting Records

Data forms can be used to selectively look at certain records based on a criterion by following these steps:

1. Click a cell in the table.

2. Click the Form icon in the Quick Access Toolbar or press Alt+D, then O.

3. In the form, click Criteria and enter the criteria you want to use, such as City=Oakland, as shown in Figure 2-24.

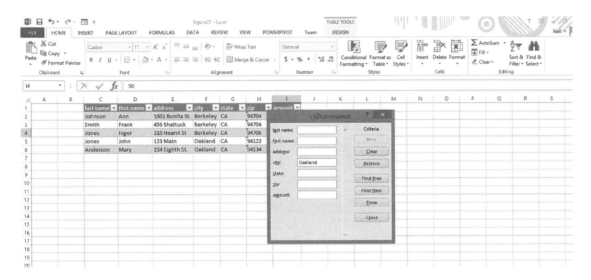

Figure 2-24. *Using a data form to select records based on a criterion*

4. Then click Find Next, and Find Previous will only show rows that meet the designated criteria.

Summary

This chapter has shown you how to import data into Excel. Figures 2-1, 2-2, 2-4, 2-5, 2-6, 2-7, 2-9, and 2-10 illustrate different ways of representing the same data. Excel can read all these formats, with the exception of JSON, which can be imported by converting it to XML as an intermediate step. You also saw how to use Tables in Excel as flat files. Chapter 3 will demonstrate how to use Pivot Tables to extract summary data from large datasets. Chapter 4 will show you how to set up relational data models.

CHAPTER 3

▬ ▬ ▬

Pivot Tables and Pivot Charts

This chapter covers extracting summary data from a single table, using Pivot Tables and Pivot Charts. The chapter also describes how to import data from the Azure Data Marketplace, using Pivot Tables. Chapter 4 will show how to extract summary data from multiple tables, using the Excel Data Model.

Recommended Pivot Tables in Excel 2013

Excel 2013 tries to anticipate your needs by recommending conditional formatting, charts, tools, and Pivot Tables. When data is highlighted or Ctrl+Q is pressed with any cell in the data range selected, a Quick Analysis Lens button is displayed at the lower right of the range. Clicking the lens will show the Analysis Tool window, which displays various conditional formatting options, as shown in Figure 3-1. Moving the cursor over a conditional formatting option will show a preview of that conditional formatting in the data. Clicking the Tables tab at the top right of the Analysis Tool window will result in several suggested Pivot Tables being shown. Hovering over each Pivot Table presents a preview, as shown in Figure 3-2.

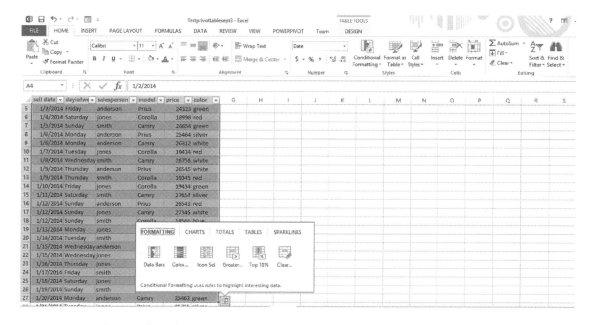

Figure 3-1. *Analysis Tool window*

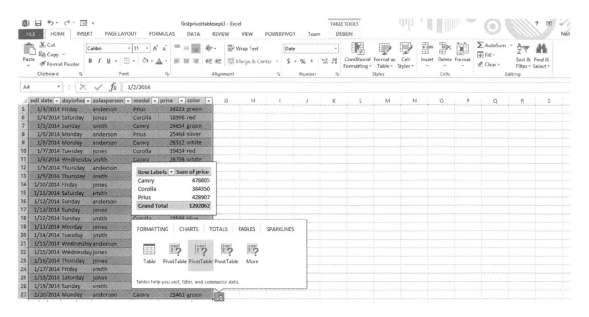

Figure 3-2. *Pivot Table preview*

Defining a Pivot Table

This section covers how to define a Pivot Table based on a simple transaction table of hypothetical Toyota sales data that lists transactions, including date of sale, model, salesperson, color, and selling price, as shown in Figure 3-3. Tables on which Pivot Tables are based should contain both numeric data and category fields, so that the numeric data can be sliced and diced by categories.

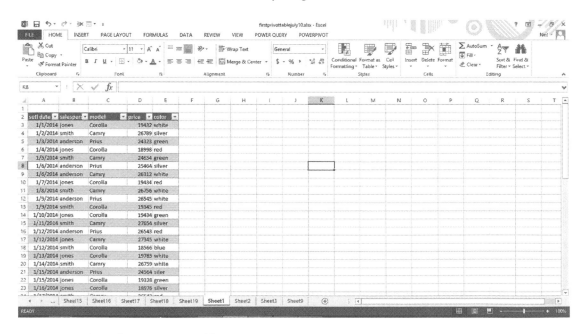

Figure 3-3. *Auto sales transaction table*

Creating a Pivot Table doesn't change the underlying data; rather, it takes a snapshot of the data. When the underlying data is changed, the Pivot Table does not automatically refresh. To refresh, click anywhere within the Pivot Table to highlight the Pivot Table Tools Analyze tab and click Refresh.

Defining Questions

It is good practice to think through what questions you want answered by the Pivot Table. Some typical questions would be the following:

- What are the average sales per day?

- Who is the best performing salesperson?

- What days of the week have the most sales?

- What months have the highest sales?

Creating a Pivot Table

The steps to define a Pivot Table are as follows:

1. Make sure that the underlying data is in table format, with the first row showing the field names, and that the data is surrounded by blank rows and columns or starts in row 1 or column A. Press Ctrl+T to define the data, as a table as shown in Figure 3-3.

2. Click anywhere within the table and highlight the Insert tab. Click PivotTable. The screen shown in Figure 3-4 will appear. Note that the current table is selected and that by default, the Pivot Table will be placed in a new worksheet. Click OK.

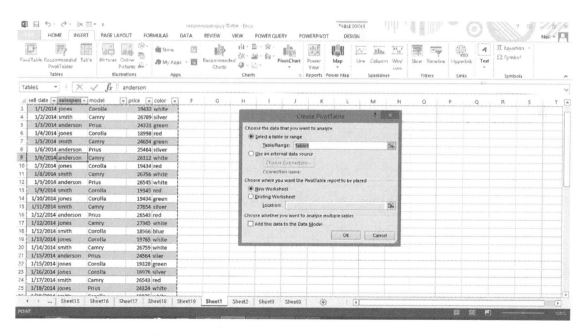

Figure 3-4. *Create PivotTable dialog*

3. At this point, you have to think through what type of data you want to extract. We
    will start with a summary of sales per day, with a breakout of models sold per day.
    We will do this by dragging sell date to the Columns box, model to Rows, and price
    to Values, as shown in Figure 3-5. Note that the default display is Sum of price.

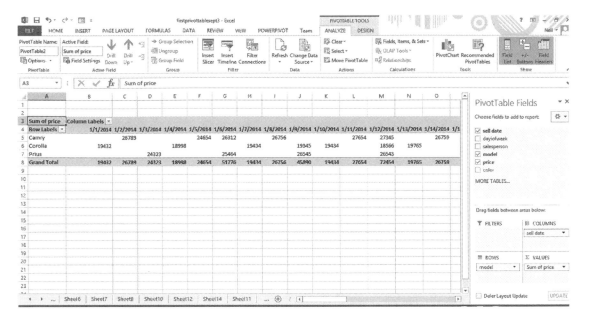

Figure 3-5. *Basic Pivot Table showing count of car sales by model*

4. To change Sum of price to Count of price, right-click cell A3 or pull down the
    arrow on Count of price under Values and select "Summarize Values by" and
    count. The result is shown in Figure 3-6.

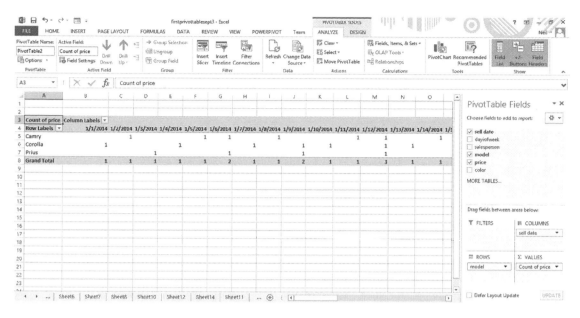

Figure 3-6. *Pivot Table showing value of car sales by model*

Changing the Pivot Table

It is very easy to make changes to the Pivot Table. To change the horizontal axis from dates to salesperson, simply click sell date from the Columns box back and select "remove field." Then drag salesperson from the Fields list to the Columns box. The result is shown in Figure 3-7.

Figure 3-7. *Pivot Table showing sales by model and salesperson*

Creating a Breakdown of Sales by Salesperson for Each Day

The Pivot Table can be modified to show the sales by salesperson and model for each day. Simply drag the model field to the Columns box and salesperson and sell date fields to the Rows box, so that both sell date and salesperson are shown in the Rows box. The results are shown in Figure 3-8.

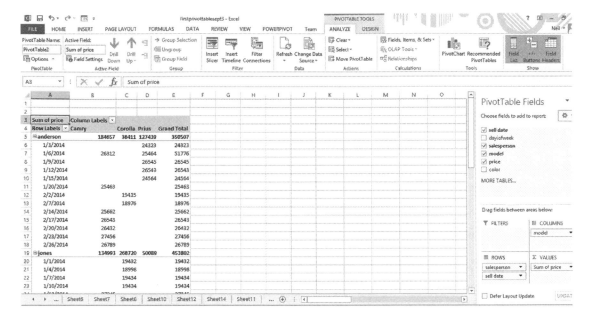

Figure 3-8. *Pivot Table showing breakdown by salesperson and model for each day*

Showing Sales by Month

To display a sales report by month, right-click any cell in the sell date column and select Months from the Grouping window, as shown in Figure 3-9, and click OK.

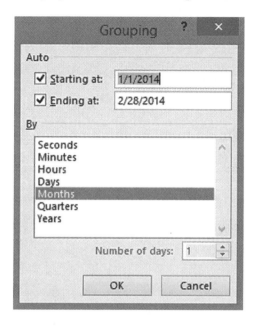

Figure 3-9. *Dialog to select grouping by month*

The resulting Pivot Table is shown in Figure 3-10.

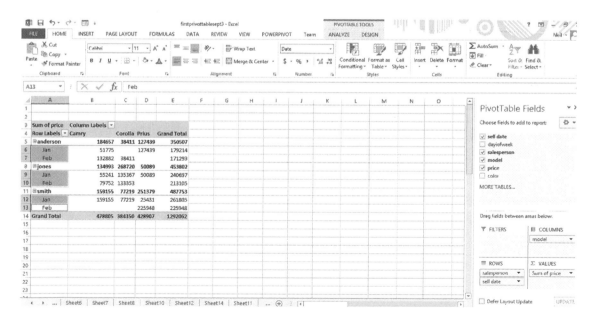

Figure 3-10. *Pivot Table showing sales by salesperson and model by month*

Creating a Pivot Chart

To create a Pivot Chart from a Pivot Table, with the Pivot Table displayed on the screen, do the following:

1. Go to the Pivot Table Tools Analyze tab and select Pivot Chart.

2. From the Insert Chart pop-up shown in Figure 3-11, select the type of chart desired and click OK. For this example, we will use a stacked column chart.

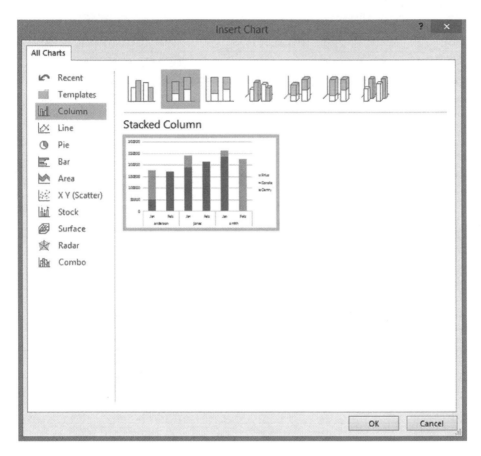

Figure 3-11. *Insert Chart dialog*

3. The result will be displayed as shown in Figure 3-12.

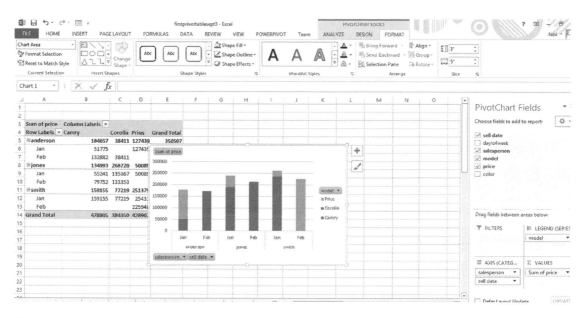

Figure 3-12. *Pivot Chart with Pivot Table*

Adjusting Subtotals and Grand Totals

The subtotals can be adjusted on the Pivot Table Tools Design tab. Click Subtotals to see the options.

- Do not show subtotals
- Show all subtotals at bottom of group
- Show all subtotals at top of group

Click Grand Totals to see the following options:

- Off for rows and columns
- On for rows and columns
- On for rows only
- On for columns only

Analyzing Sales by Day of Week

It can be useful to analyze sales by day of the week. In this example, we have added a column for day of week, using the following steps:

1. Insert a column to the left of salesperson. Name the new column "day of week."

2. Enter the following formula in cell B3, to extract the day of week:

    =TEXT(A3,"dddd")

3. The formula will be automatically copied down the column, because this is a table. The result is as shown in Figure 3-13.

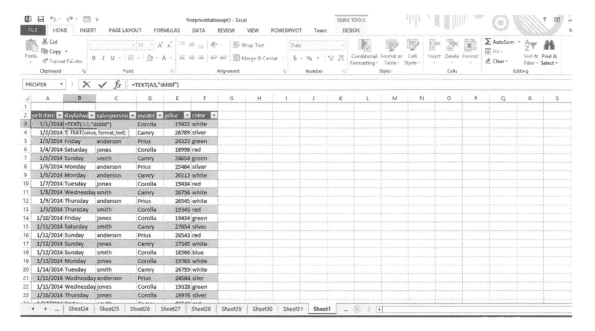

Figure 3-13. *Extracting day of week*

4. Save the spreadsheet.

5. On the Insert tab, click PivotTable. Click OK in the Create PivotTable pop-up window to accept the default.

6. If necessary, click Refresh on the Pivot Table Analyze tab to display the new column.

7. On the PivotTable Fields tab, drag model to the Columns box, day of week to Rows, and Sum of price to Values to get the Pivot Table shown in Figure 3-14.

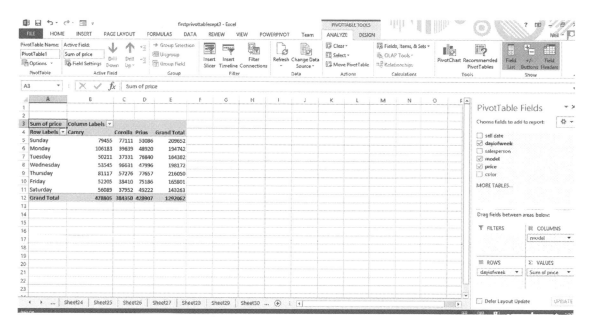

Figure 3-14. *Pivot Table of sales by day of week and model*

Creating a Pivot Chart of Sales by Day of Week

To get a visual representation of sales by day of the week, create a Pivot Chart from a Pivot Table. With the Pivot Table displayed on the screen, do the following:

1. Go to the Pivot Table Tools Analyze tab and select Pivot Chart.

2. From the Insert Chart pop-up shown in Figure 3-15, select the type of chart desired.

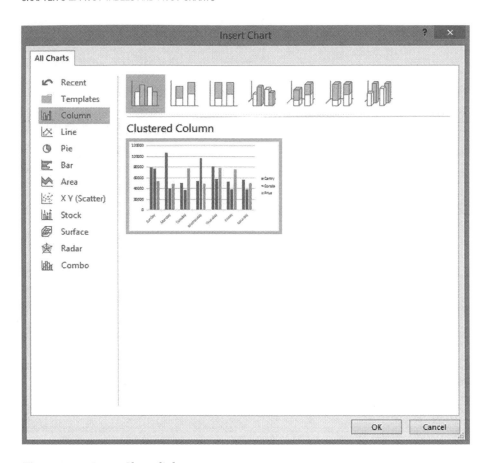

Figure 3-15. *Insert Chart dialog*

3. If a clustered column chart is selected, the results will be as shown in Figure 3-16.

Figure 3-16. *Pivot Chart for sales by day of week*

Using Slicers

Slicers can be used to filter data and to zoom in on specific field values in the Pivot Table. To set up a slicer, do the following:

1. Go to the Pivot Table Tools Analyze tab and select Insert Slicer.

2. From the Insert Slicers pop-up window, select the fields that you want to slice, such as salesperson and date, and click OK.

3. The result is shown in Figure 3-17, which displays the sales by salesperson for each model and date...A specific salesperson can be selected, and the slicer menu can be selected to view sales for that salesperson.

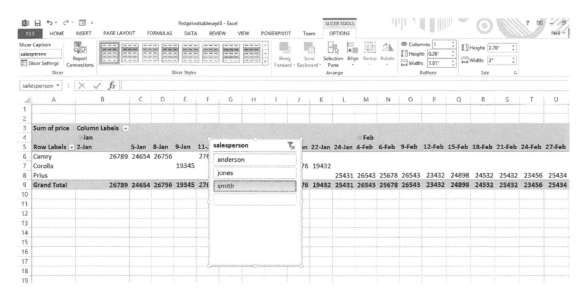

Figure 3-17. *Filtering results using salesperson slicer*

Adding a Time Line

A time line can be added to slice by time intervals. To add a time line, do the following:

1. From the Pivot Table Tool Analyze tab, select Insert Timeline. Select sell date in the Insert Timeline window and click OK. The time period for the time line can be selected by clicking the down arrow at the upper right of the Timeline window to select years, quarters, months, or days.

2. As seen in Figure 3-18, Timeline and Slicer work together. A specific salesperson and date can be selected to view sales by that salesperson on that date.

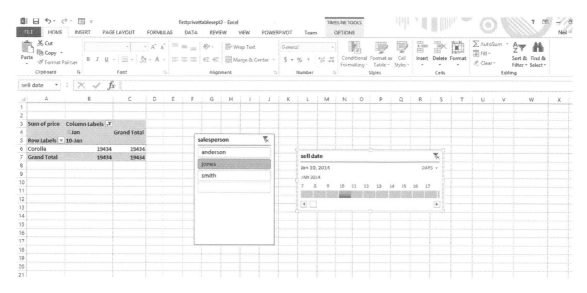

Figure 3-18. *Filtering data with a time line plus salesperson slicer*

Importing Pivot Table Data from the Azure Marketplace

Data can be imported into a Pivot Table from the Azure Marketplace, which includes a wide variety of data, such as demographic, environmental, financial, retail, and sports. Some of the data is free, and some is not. The following example shows how to access free data.

1. Go to the Azure Marketplace web site at datamarket.azure.com/browse/data. The screen shown in Figure 3-19 will appear as of August 2015.

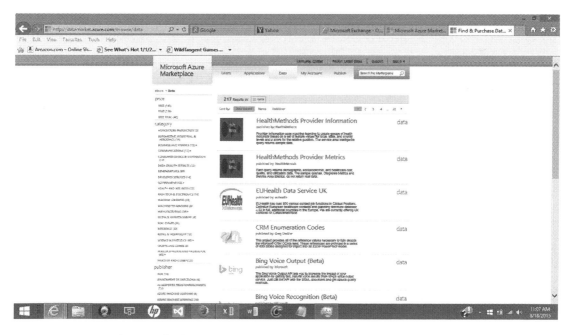

Figure 3-19. *Azure data market browse screen*

2.   The first time you use the site, you may be asked to fill in account information
      and to create a free account ID. If you already have a free Microsoft account, such
      as a Hotmail.com or Outlook.com account, you can use that.

3.   Click Data at the top of the screen. The screen shown in Figure 3-20 will appear.

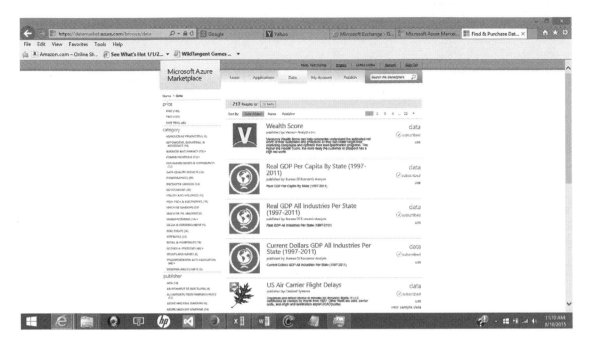

Figure 3-20. *Azure Marketplace*

4.   Scroll through the data sources. You may have to go through an additional sign-
      up process to use free data.

5.   For this example, we will use Real GDP Per Capita By State (1997–2011), as
      shown in Figure 3-21. If prompted, enter your Microsoft ID and agree to the
      terms of use.

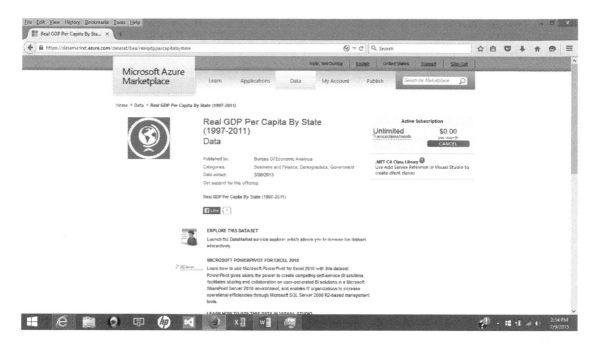

Figure 3-21. *Real GDP all industries per state database*

6. Click Explore this Dataset in the middle of the screen.

7. The data will be displayed, as shown in Figure 3-22. Note, in the upper-right corner of the screen, the Download Options of Excel (CSV), PowerPivot 2010, and PowerPivot 2013. Select PowerPivot 2013.

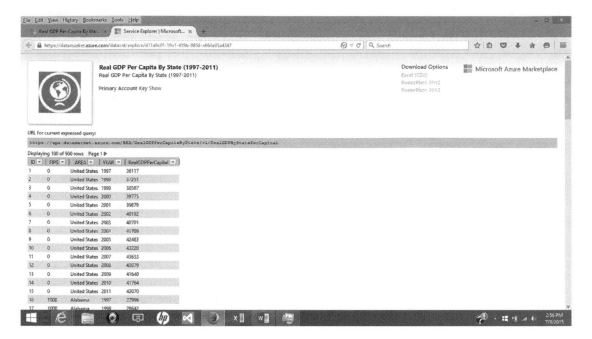

Figure 3-22. *Display of real GDP per capita records*

8. You will be prompted to save the file. Click OK. The file will appear in the download section of your web browser. What you will see now depends on which web browser you are using. To save the file and open in Excel, click whatever prompts appear. If using Firefox, double-click the file name to start the process. If you are prompted to select the program to use to open the file, choose Excel.

9. A pop-up window will appear, as shown in Figure 3-23, asking for how you want to view the data. Select Pivot Table Report, click OK, and wait for the data to download.

Figure 3-23. *Import Data dialog*

10. If a pop-up appears asking for your account key, enter your Microsoft username (e.g., a Hotmail or Outlook.com e-mail address).

11. Start designing the Pivot Table. Drag year to the Columns box, drag area to the Row box, and Real GDP to Values, as shown in Figure 3-24.

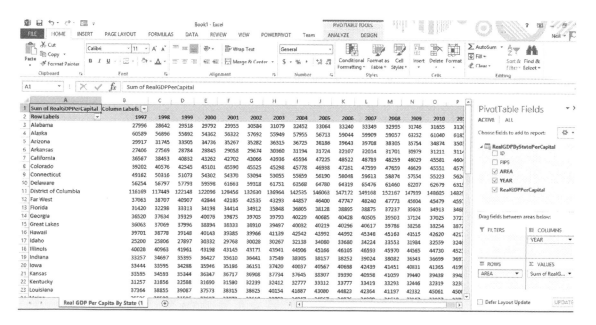

Figure 3-24. *Real GDP data imported into Excel*

12. To use a slicer to filter the data, click Insert Slicer on the Pivot Table Tools Analyze tab. Select the Area field and click OK. On the Slicer menu, select a state, such as California, to view its real GDP per capita, as shown in Figure 3-25.

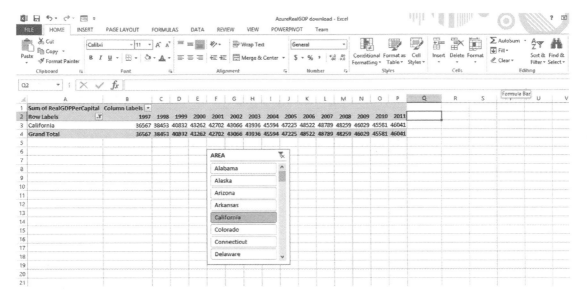

Figure 3-25. *Real GDP data filtered by slicer*

Summary

This chapter showed how to use Pivot Tables and Pivot Charts based on a single table and how to import data from the Microsoft Azure Marketplace. Chapter 4 will show how to use the Excel Data Model to extract data from multiple tables.

CHAPTER 4

■ ■ ■

Building a Data Model

This chapter will cover the Excel Data Model also known as the PowerPivot Data Model. PowerPivot for Excel 2013 is based on the tabular engine of SQL Server Analysis Services 2012 running inside Excel. The Data Model allows relating of multiple tables. It runs completely in memory and compresses data so that it can process millions of rows.

The Excel Data Model is a collection of tables, including the relationships between them. The Data Model provides the structure for Power BI. This chapter will demonstrate how to use Pivot Tables to extract summary information from multiple tables in a Data Model. The examples used will progress from the simple to the more complex.

Enabling PowerPivot

PowerPivot is included with Excel 2013, but it is not enabled by default. To enable PowerPivot, follow these steps:

1.   Click the File tab to see the Backstage view.

2.   Click Options at the bottom of the left pane.

3.   Select Add-Ins on the left pane.

4.   At the bottom of the window, pull down the arrow after Manage, select COM Add-ins, and click Go, as shown in Figure 4-1.

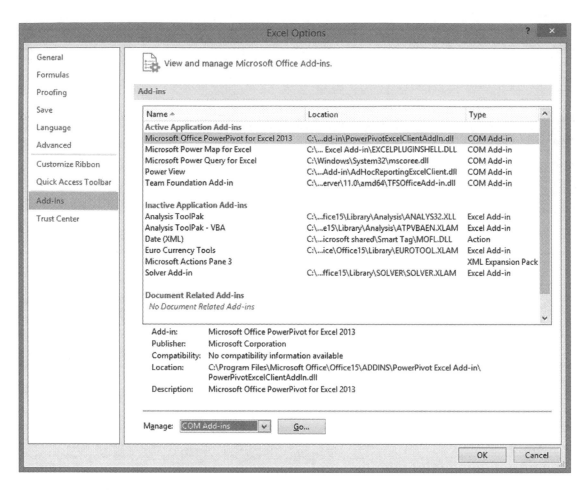

Figure 4-1. *Excel Options screen*

5.   Check Microsoft Office PowerPivot for Excel 2013, Microsoft Power Map for Excel, and Power View, as shown in Figure 4-2, and click OK.

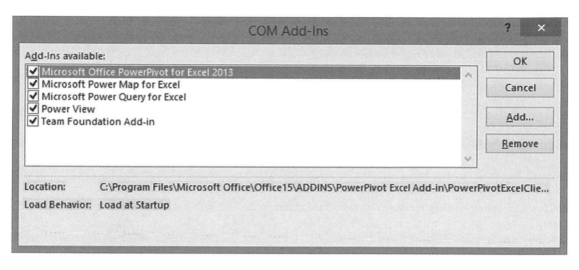

Figure 4-2. *COM Add-Ins dialog*

Relational Databases

Until a few years ago, relational databases were the most widely used type of database. In the last few years, NoSQL (or nonrelational) databases have become popular for log data and other types of big data. NoSQL databases will be covered more extensively in future chapters. Still, today, the majority of transactional business data is stored in relational databases.

One of the principles of relational database design is avoiding repeating fields. If repeating fields are encountered, the data is normalized by creating other tables, as described in Chapter 1. For instance, in a personnel example, the primary key of the employee table would be the employee Social Security number, because it is unique, and it is required for financial reporting. The employee would be assigned to a department, but only a department code would be stored in the employee table. The department code would be a foreign key that would point to the appropriate record in the department table, which would have other information, such as the department office, department manager, and phone number. Thus, the department information would not have to be repeated for each employee record.

Database Terminology

The following terms are commonly used to describe relational databases and the relationships between tables within a database.

- A *field* is the smallest unit of data in a table. Fields are stored in columns in Excel tables.

- A *record* is all of the data or information about one person or one thing. In Excel, a record is a row in a table.

- A *table* is a collection of related data stored in a structured format within a database. It consists of fields (columns) and records (rows).

- A *database* is a collection of tables.

- The *primary key* of a relational table is a field (or fields) that uniquely identifies each record in the table. For data involving people, especially data that requires tax reporting, the most common primary key is a Social Security number. It is, of course, important to have proper security when dealing with personal data such as Social Security numbers.

- A *foreign key* is a field or fields in one table that uniquely identifies a row of another table.

- A *candidate key* is a field or fields in a table that can uniquely identify any record without referring to any other data. Each table may have one or more candidate keys, but one candidate key is selected as the primary key. This is usually the best among the candidate keys.

- When a key is composed of more than one column, it is known as a *composite key*.

- A *relationship* allows accessing data from multiple tables, based on a key field.

- *Normalization* is the process of organizing the tables in a relational database to minimize redundancy. Normalization often involves dividing large tables into smaller tables and defining relationships between them.

- *Third Normal Form (3NF)*, defined by relational database model inventor E. F. Codd, eliminates fields not dependent on the primary key. To be in Third Normal Form, each field in a table must depend on the primary key, and only the primary key, of that table. This is called eliminating **transitive tendencies**, where one field depends on another field that is not the primary key.

- A *source table* is the table wherein the relationship starts. In the example in the following section, the employee table is the source table.

- The *related table* is the table that contains the values to look up. In the following example, the department table is the related table.

Creating a Data Model from Excel Tables

This section will start with a simple example, to illustrate the principles of relating tables. In this example, a Data Model will be created from two small tables: employee and department. The tables are normalized, meaning that repeating fields have been eliminated. Instead of recording all the information about a single department in the employee record, only a department code is used. Then a relationship is defined between the employee and department table, so that the department information can be extracted from the department table.

A Pivot Table can be used to extract meaningful information from a Data Model. To create a Pivot Table that draws on data from both tables to show average salary by department, do the following:

1. Define each group of data as a table by clicking inside the table and pressing Ctrl+T.

2. Click anywhere in the table and click the Table Tools Design tab. On the left side of the ribbon, type in a table name, in this case, *employees*, as shown in Figure 4-3. Also, rename the departments.

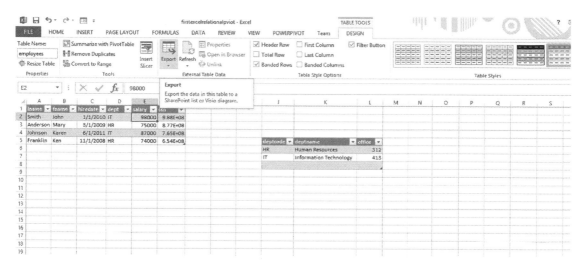

Figure 4-3. *Employee and department tables*

3. Highlight the employee table. Go to the Insert tab and select Pivot Table. In the Create PivotTable dialog, select *Add this data to the Data Model* and click OK, as shown in Figure 4-4.

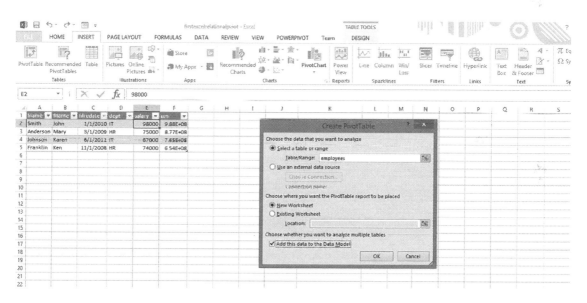

Figure 4-4. *Create PivotTable dialog*

4. In the PivotTable Fields pane, click All (at the upper right), to see both tables, as shown in Figure 4-5. Drag the deptname field from the department table to the columns box. Drag Sum of salary from the employees table to values. Note the prompt "Relationships between tables may be needed." Click Create.

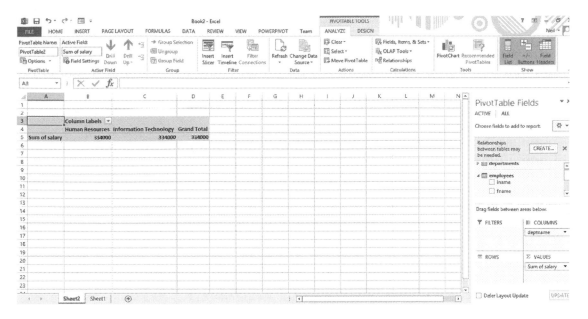

Figure 4-5. *PivotTable showing total salaries by department*

5. As shown in Figure 4-6, select employees as the first table and dept as the foreign key. Select departments as the second table and deptcode as the primary key. Click OK. Note that the field names, as defined by the column headings, do not have to be the same.

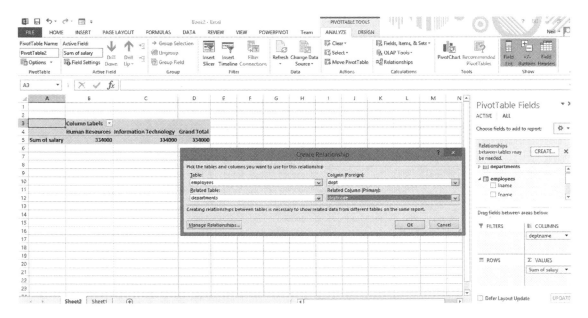

Figure 4-6. *Create Relationship dialog*

6. Drag lname to the Rows box. The resulting Pivot Table, as shown in Figure 4-7, will display the sum of salaries by department.

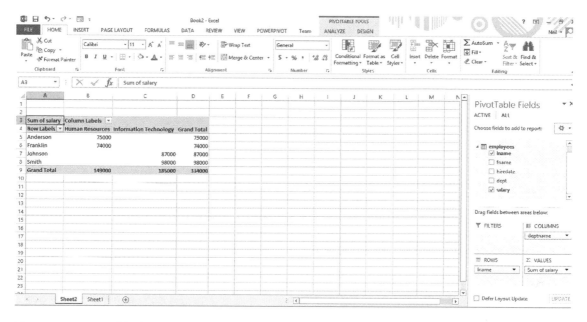

Figure 4-7. *PivotTable showing employee salary by department*

7. To see instead the average salary by department, first remove the lname field from the Rows box and then in the PivotTable Fields pane, click the drop-down arrow next to Sum of salary in the Values box. Select value field setting and then average to see the average salary by department, as shown in Figure 4-8.

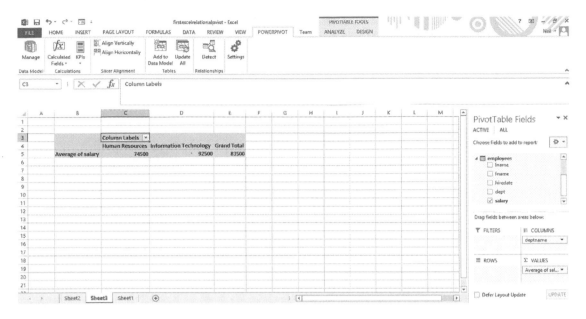

Figure 4-8. PivotTable showing average salary by department

8. This example showed how to relate two tables, employees and departments, using department code. dept is a foreign key in the employees table, and deptcode is the primary key for the departments table. The Pivot Table relates the two tables.

Loading Data Directly into the Data Model

In this example, data will be loaded directly into the Data Model using an example from Microsoft's Northwind Access Database. This example demonstrates running PowerPivot on top of Excel.

To load data directly into the Data Model, do the following:

1. Click the PowerPivot tab to open the ribbon.

2. Click the Manage button at the top-left end of the ribbon.

3. Once the PowerPivot window is open, you can load data by clicking *From Database* in the Get External Data group. This provides a choice of database sources, as shown in Figure 4-9. For this example, *From Access* will be selected.

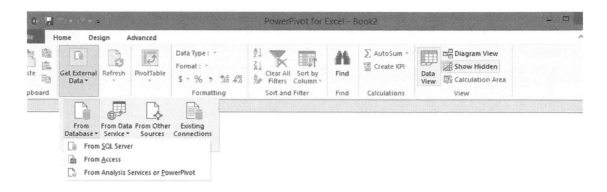

Figure 4-9. *PowerPivot Get External Data group*

4. In the Table Import Wizard dialog, click the Browse button to find the Access file you want to import. For this example, Database1 in the documents folder will be selected. This file is available from the Apress web site.

5. Click *Test Connection*. If the test is successful, click Next.

6. PowerPivot opens the Table Import Wizard, as shown in Figure 4-10, to step you through the process of loading data. Choose *Select from a list of tables and views to choose the data to import*. Click Next.

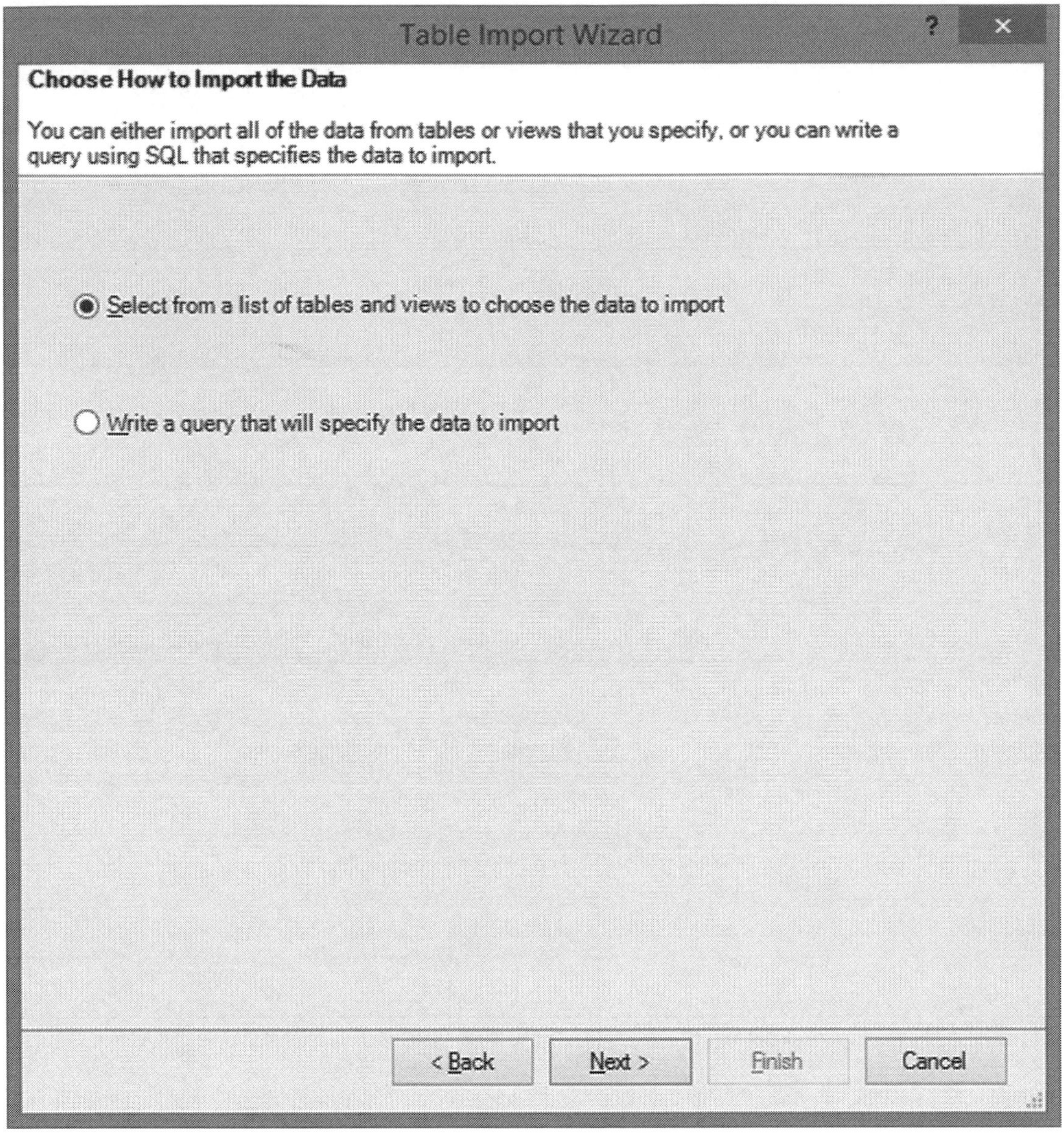

Figure 4-10. *Table Import Wizard*

7. Click the top-left box to select all tables, as shown in Figure 4-11. Note that in the lower right corner of the dialog, there is an option to *Preview & Filter*. This option can be used to select a subset of data from very large datasets. In this example, all rows in all tables will be imported. Click Finish to complete the import.

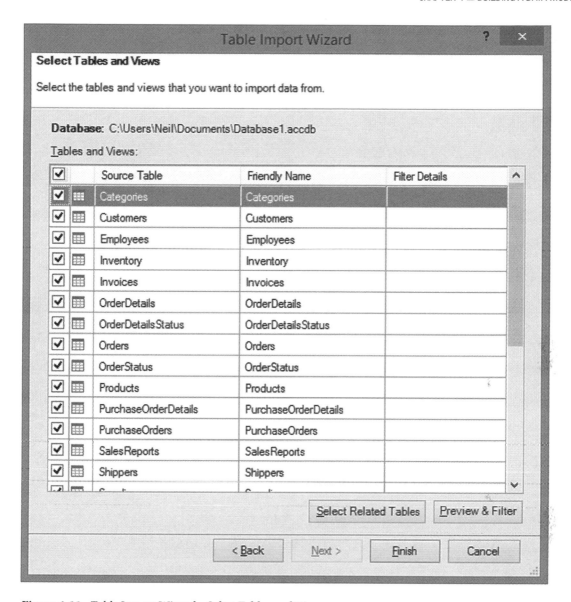

Figure 4-11. *Table Import Wizard—Select Tables and Views*

Relationships are automatically loaded into the data model, if they are present in the imported data. Note that PowerPivot tables are read-only, so that the data cannot be changed.

To view relationships, go to the PowerPivot tab and select Manage to open the PowerPivot window. Then click the PowerPivot Diagram View at the right end of the ribbon to see the relationships between tables, and click Finish to complete the import, as shown in Figure 4-12.

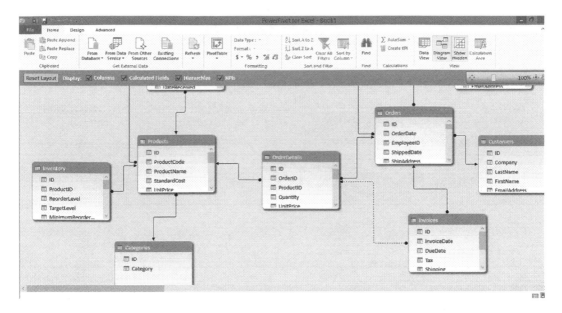

Figure 4-12. *Diagram View*

Creating a Pivot Table from Two Tables

In this example, a Pivot Table will be created, based on the inventory and products tables. Notice in Figure 4-12 that the two tables are linked, based on product code. The Inventory table includes the on-hand data for each item in inventory, with a primary key of ProductCode. To find the full product name, a lookup has to be performed in the product table, based on product ID. To create a Pivot Table based on these two tables, do the following:

1. Click Pivot Table on the File tab in the PowerPivot window and select PivotTable from the menu.

2. Click OK to put the Pivot Table in a new worksheet.

3. Click the arrow next to the products table in the Pivot Table Fields pane and drag the ProductName field to the Rows box. Then scroll up to go to the inventory table, click the left arrow to show the fields, and drag OnHand to the Values box. The results are shown in Figure 4-13, which indicates the sum of the on-hand values for each product.

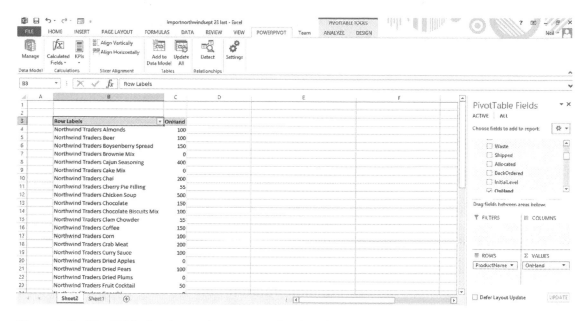

Figure 4-13. *PivotTable showing product name and on-hand quantity*

Creating a Pivot Table from Multiple Tables

This example will demonstrate how to create Pivot Tables from more than two tables, based on the relationships between the tables. It will use the PowerPivotTutorialSample spreadsheet from the Contoso database, which can be downloaded from the following URL: Tinyurl.com/PowerPivotSamples.

A Pivot Table accessing fields from multiple related tables can be created by following these steps:

1. Download the PowerPivotTutorialSample spreadsheet from the preceding URL.

2. Click the Manage icon on the PowerPivot tab to open the PowerPivot window. Then click Diagram View to see the diagram of relationships, as shown in Figure 4-14. Note that the arrows show relations in a somewhat imprecise manner: using the scrollbar to scroll through the field names does not change the position of the arrow. A clearer way to see relationships is to minimize the PowerPivot window and click Relationships on the Data tab, to see the actual field names that are linked in the Manage Relationships screen, as shown in Figure 4-15. Note that you can also see a similar view by clicking Manage Relationships on the Design tab of the PowerPivot window.

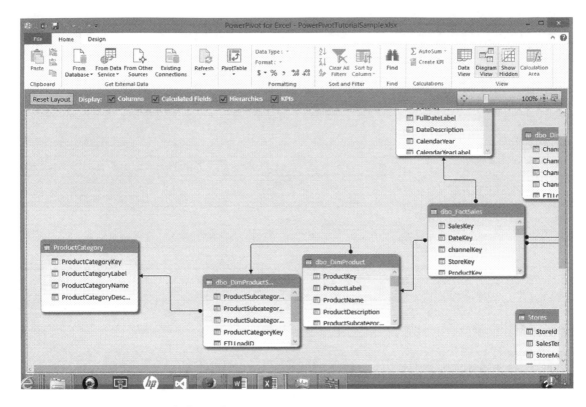

Figure 4-14. *Diagram view of relationships*

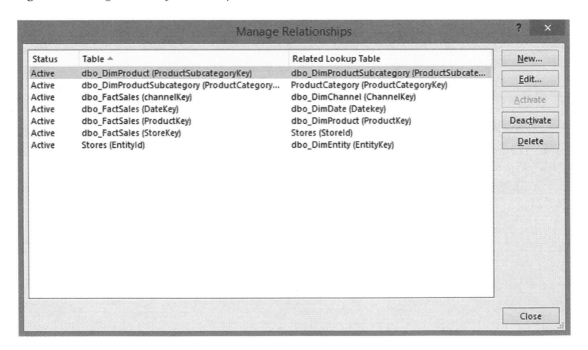

Figure 4-15. *Manage Relationships screen*

3. To create a Pivot Table based on related fields, select the PowerPivot tab and Click Manage. If the Diagram View is still displayed, click Data View. Notice the tabs at the bottom of the screen that show the tables included in this example. A PivotTable will be created that links the dbo_FactSales table with the dbo_DimProduct table and the dbo_DimDate table. The purpose of the Pivot Table is to analyze product sales by date.

4. Click Pivot Table and select Pivot Table from the drop-down. In the Create PivotTable dialog, accept the default of New Worksheet by clicking OK.

5. In the PivotTable Fields pane, the tables will be shown preceded by a right-facing arrow. Click the right-facing arrow to see the fields in that table. Scroll to the dbo_DimProduct table and click the arrow. Drag the ProductName field to the Rows box. Click the arrow to the left of the dbo_DimProduct table to suppress the fields display. Scroll to the dbo_DimDate table and click the arrow, to see the fields. Drag the FullDateLabel field to the Columns box. Click the arrow to suppress the fields. Scroll to the dbo_FactSales table and click the arrow, to see the fields. Drag the SalesQuantity field to the Values box. The results will be shown in Figure 4-16. It is possible to link fields from multiple tables because of the relationships shown in Figure 4-15.

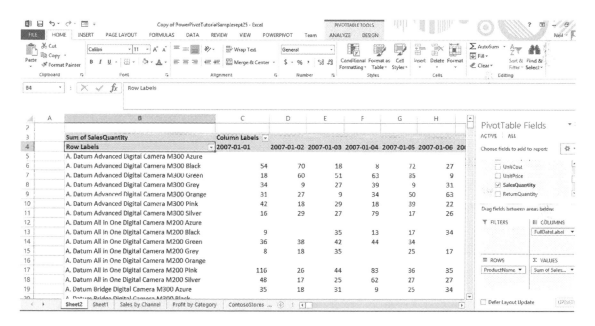

Figure 4-16. *PivotTable showing sales by product and date*

6. To further modify the Pivot Table by viewing sales by product by year, remove FullDateLabel from the Columns box and replace it with CalenderYear from the DimDate table. The results are shown in Figure 4-17.

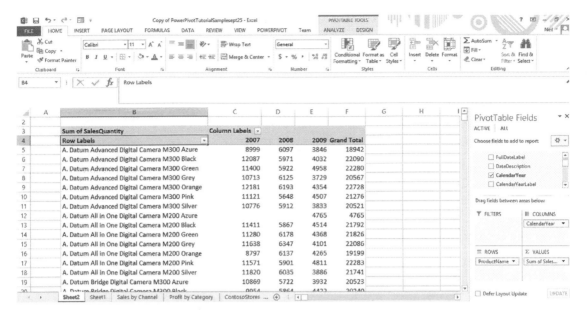

Figure 4-17. *PivotTable showing sales by product and year*

Adding Calculated Columns

Calculated columns can be added to a table in PowerPivot, using Data Analysis Expressions (DAX). Regular Excel formulas are based on cells. By contrast, DAX formulas are based on columns. DAX will be covered more extensively in future chapters. This example will show how to set up a calculated column. To add a calculated column, take the following steps:

1. Select the PowerPivot tab and click Manage.

2. Select the dbo_FactSales table by clicking the tab at the bottom of the display.

3. Scroll to the right to the TotalProfit column. Note that to the right, the column heading is Add Column.

4. Select any cell in that column and type = to start a formula.

5. Create an extended price column that is the product of unit price times quantity. To do this, after typing =, click the SalesQuantity column, type *, and then click the unit price quantity. The formula is shown in Figure 4-18, in the formula bar: =[SalesQuantity]*[UnitPrice]

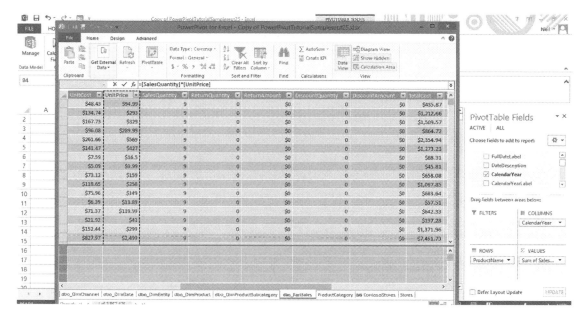

Figure 4-18. *Adding calculated column*

6. Then press Enter to complete the formula.

7. To rename the column, right-click the column heading, select Rename Column, and name it "extended price." The results are shown in Figure 4-19. Note that the values in the new column are the same as the TotalSales but are based on a formula.

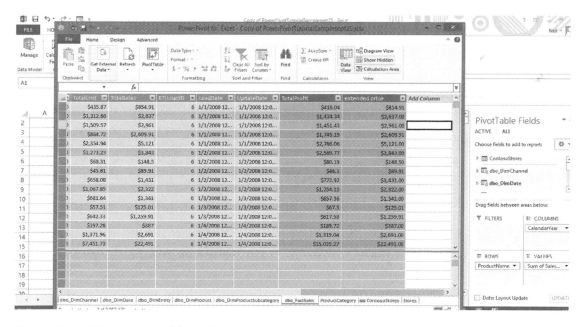

Figure 4-19. *Column renamed "extended price"*

When using PowerPivot calculated columns, all cells share the same formulas. It is not possible to use formulas involving individual cells. Aggregation functions such as SUM(), Average(), and COUNT() can apply to an entire column, to extract summary data.

Adding Calculated Fields to the Data Model

This example will show how to design a Pivot Table that shows sales quantity by product by month, using calculated fields. To do this follows these steps:

1. Click the Pivot Table icon and accept the default of a new sheet.

2. From the dbo_DimDate table, drag the CalenderMonthLabel field to the Rows box.

3. From the ProductCategory table, drag theProductCategoryName field to the Columns box.

4. From the dbo_FactSales table, drag the SalesQuantity field to the Values box.

To add a calculated field to the data model, take the following steps:

1. On the PowerPivot tab, click Calculated Field.

2. Click new Calculated Field.

3. From the drop-down, select the table on which the calculated field will be based, in this case, dbo_FactSales.

4. Name the calculated field "profitability."

5. Click the Fx icon, to see the functions. Many of the functions are similar to basic Excel functions.

6. Scroll down to SUM(), as shown in Figure 4-20, and click OK.

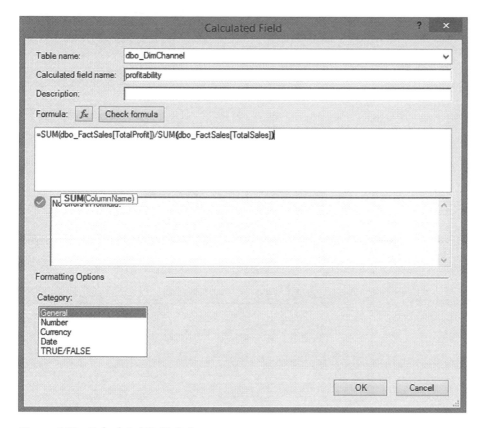

Figure 4-20. *Calculated Field dialog*

7. Following the left parenthesis, start typing the name of the table to use, in this case, dbo_FactSales. The fields for that table will then be displayed. Scroll down to dbo_FactSales[totalprofit] and double click. Type the closing parenthesis. Then type / and sum(dbo_FactsSales[totalsales] and close the parenthesis.

8. Then Click *check formula*. If the formula tests OK, click OK.

The calculated field column will appear as shown in Figure 4-21.

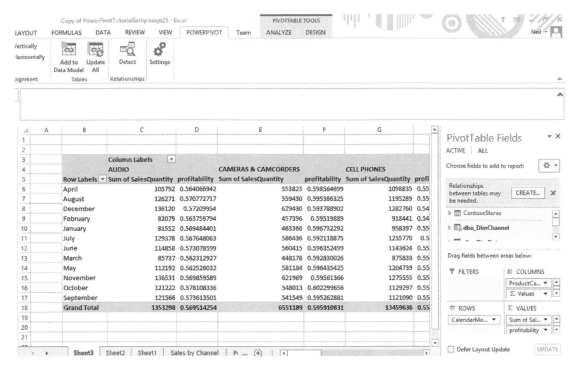

Figure 4-21. *PivotTable showing profitability and sales by month*

Summary

This chapter provided an introduction to building a Data Model in PowerPivot. In future chapters, more advanced features of the Data Model will be explored. Figure 4-22 shows the number of rows downloaded for each table. Notice that the dbo_FactSales table has almost 4 million rows. That number of rows is supported in PowerPivot but not in Excel.

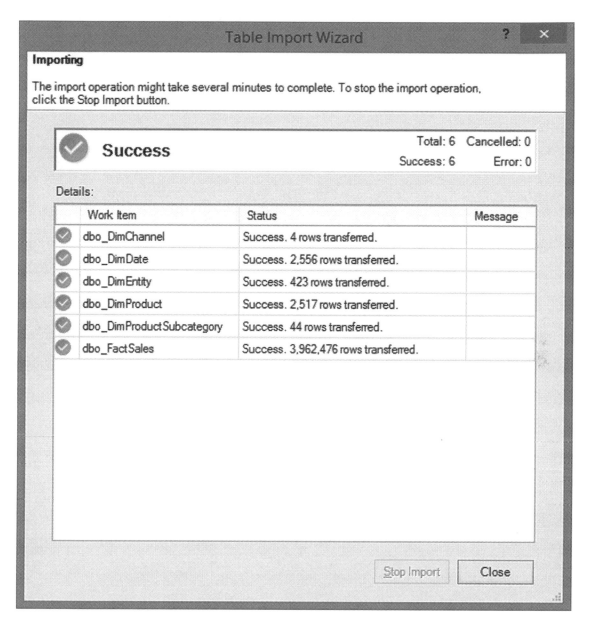

Figure 4-22. *Table Import Wizard showing number of rows imported*

CHAPTER 5

Using SQL in Excel

This chapter covers using SQL (Structured Query Language) in Excel to import and manipulate subsets of large data files and to extract summary statistics.

History of SQL

SQL was first developed by IBM in the early 1970s and was called SEQUEL (Structured English Query Language). It was used to manipulate and retrieve data from early IBM relational database management systems (RDBMS). Because of trademark conflicts, SEQUEL was shortened to SQL. It was later implemented in other relational database management systems by Oracle and later Microsoft. In 1986, the American National Standards Institute (ANSI) issued an SQL standard. In my opinion, the correct pronunciation is S-Q-L, but some people still pronounce it Sequel.

SQL is a declarative language, meaning that it specifies what results are wanted without defining the how. SQL consists of a Data Definition Language and a Data Manipulation Language. In Excel, mostly the query feature of the Data Manipulation Language is used, because the data definition is performed through Excel, by importing tables from other sources. SQL was originally based on the relational model, meaning that data is stored in multiple tables, based on a fixed structure.

NoSQL

As discussed in Chapter 1, the term *NoSQL* is a misnomer, because some NoSQL systems have an SQL interface. A more accurate term would be *non-relational*, or *not only SQL*. Relational databases have a fixed schema that must be defined before any data can be entered. By contrast, NoSQL databases can access data with different schemas. This is sometimes called schema on read.

NewSQL

NewSQL tries to be a compromise between relational and NoSQL systems. These systems use a relational architecture and have SQL as their primary interface but aspire to have the same scalability and flexibility as NoSQL systems.

SQL++

SQL++ is a new form of the language, which enhances traditional SQL and is based on a semi-structured data model that can access JSON data as well as traditional relational data. It is generally backward compatible with traditional SQL.

One implementation of SQL++ is N1QL (pronounced "Nickel"), which is being developed by Couchbase based on a 2014 paper by Kian Win Ong, Yannis Papakonstantinou, and Romain Vernoux entitled "The SQL++ Unifying Semi-structured Query Language, and an Expressiveness Benchmark of SQL-on-Hadoop, NoSQL and NewSQL Databases."

SQL Syntax

The mainstay of the SQL query language is the SELECT command. The syntax of that command is shown following. Note that clauses enclosed in square brackets are optional.

```
SELECT [DISTINCT] <columns list>
[AS <optional alias name for returned columns>]
FROM <table name(s)>
[WHERE <condition>]
[GROUP BY <column expression for calculating aggregates>]
[HAVING <group level filter condition>]
[ORDER BY <sort order for the results table>]
```

The SELECT clause names the columns or column expressions to be shown. An asterisk can be used to specify all columns. The FROM clause lists the table or tables to be accessed. The WHERE clause is used to provide a criteria for relating multiple tables and/or provides a row-level filter, which is used to eliminate rows that do not meet the desired condition. GROUP BY is used to arrange the results table in groups for data aggregation such as subtotaling. The HAVING clause provides a group-level filter for the results set. The ORDER BY clause is used to arrange the results table in the specified order. The methodology for doing this in PowerPivot and Excel will be demonstrated in this chapter.

When using the SELECT statement, the following questions should be addressed:

SELECT: What are the desired columns or columns expressions to be displayed?

FROM: In what tables are these columns?

WHERE: What are the conditions that link the tables? What are the selection criteria to eliminate unwanted rows?

GROUP BY: What values are to be aggregated for such purposes as subtotals?

HAVING: What conditions must each record meet to be included in the result table when using aggregation?

ORDER BY: In what order should the results be presented?

For example, the following SQL SELECT statement extracts the name and address fields from the addrlist table in which the zip code is equal to "94704."

```
SELECT name, address FROM addrlist WHERE zip="94704"
```

SQL Aggregate Functions

SQL includes various aggregate functions to allow calculating subtotals, subaverages, subcounts, etc., based on the condition in the WHERE clause.

These functions include:

COUNT(): Returns the number of non-empty rows for the conditions specified

SUM(): Returns the sum of all values in the specified columns

MIN(): Returns the lowest value in the specified column

MAX(): Returns the largest value in the specified column

AVG(): Returns the average value for the specified column

The functions can be applied to the entire table or subsets of the table, as defined by the WHERE conditions. Look at these statements, for example:

SELECT COUNT(*) FROM offices: Would return the number of rows in the offices table

SELECT COUNT(*) FROM office WHERE region="CH": Would return the number of offices in the Chicago region

SELECT SUM(sales) FROM offices: Would return the sum of sales for all rows in the offices table

SELECT SUM(sales) FROM offices where region="CH": Would return the sum of the sales field for all offices in the Chicago region

Subtotals

It would be possible to display a count of all offices in each region, using the following statement:

SELECT region, COUNT(*) FROM offices GROUP BY region

Subtotals of sales for all regions could be generated using the following statement:

SELECT region, SUM(sales) FROM offices GROUP BY region

Joining Tables

When querying multiple tables, it is best to use a WHERE clause to specify the condition for joining the tables. This is called an equijoin, because it is based on an equality test. If the WHERE clause is omitted, every row in the first table will be paired with every row in the second table. This is called the Cartesian product, or outer join of the two tables.

Importing an External Database

This example will use the Access Northwind sample database. To execute this sample, take the following steps:

1.   Click the PowerPivot tab to open the ribbon.

2.   Click the Manage button.

3.   On the PowerPivot tab, click "Get External Data" and "From Database." Select "From Access."

4.   Click Browse and select Database2, which was previously downloaded from the Northwind Database site, as shown in Figure 5-1. This file is also available for download from the Source Code/Downloads tab on the Apress book page at www.apress.com/9781484205303.

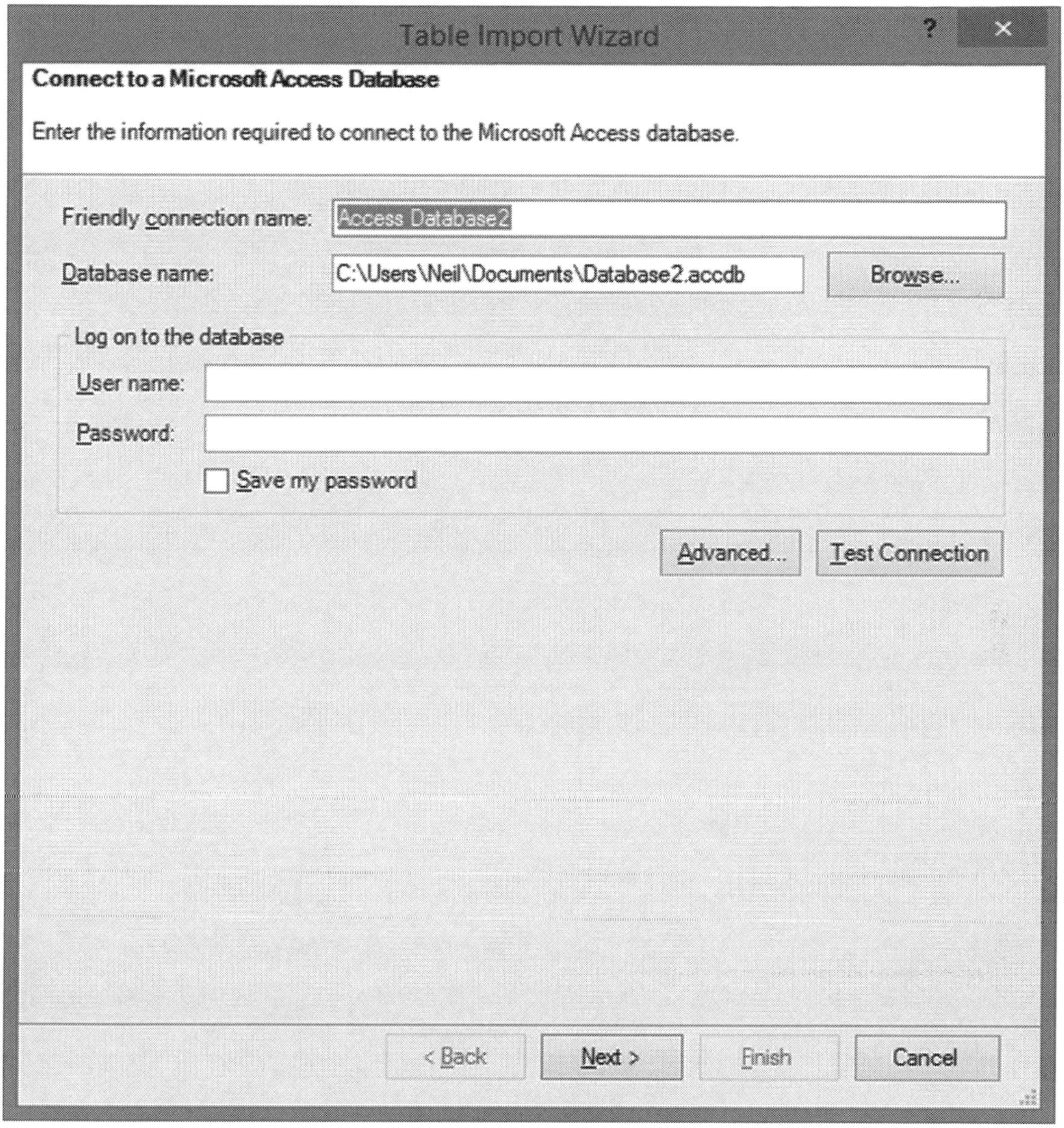

Figure 5-1. *Importing database with Table Import Wizard*

5. Click Test Connection. If the connection tests OK, click Next.

6. Select the second option, "Write a query that will specify the data to import," as shown in Figure 5-2. Click Next.

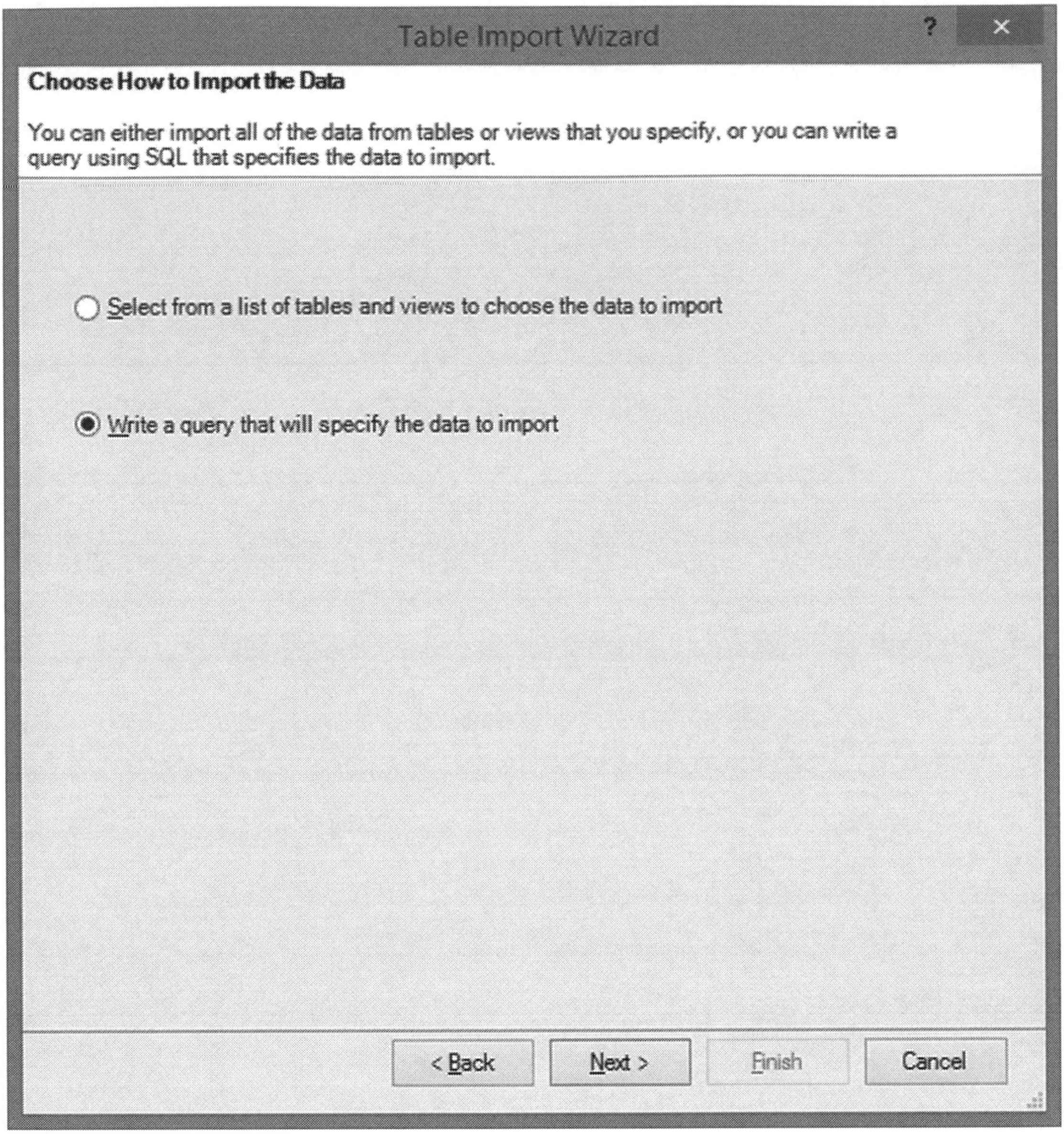

Figure 5-2. *Select "Write a query that will specify the data to import"*

Before writing a query, it is helpful to know the structure and relationships defined in the database. When importing an Access database, the relationships defined in Access are imported, as shown in Figure 5-3.

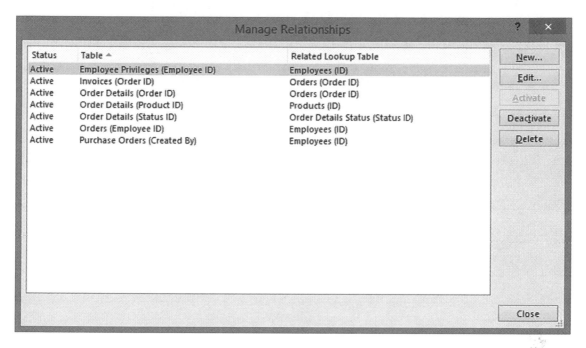

Figure 5-3. *Existing relationships*

7. The first query will import all fields from the orders and employees tables, based on the relationship shown in Figure 5-3, where the EmployeeId field in the Orders table is linked to the ID field in the Employees table. In the SQL Statement window, enter the following SQL Statement:

```
SELECT * from orders, cmployees
```

8. Then click Validate. The window will appear as shown in Figure 5-4, if the SQL is entered correctly.

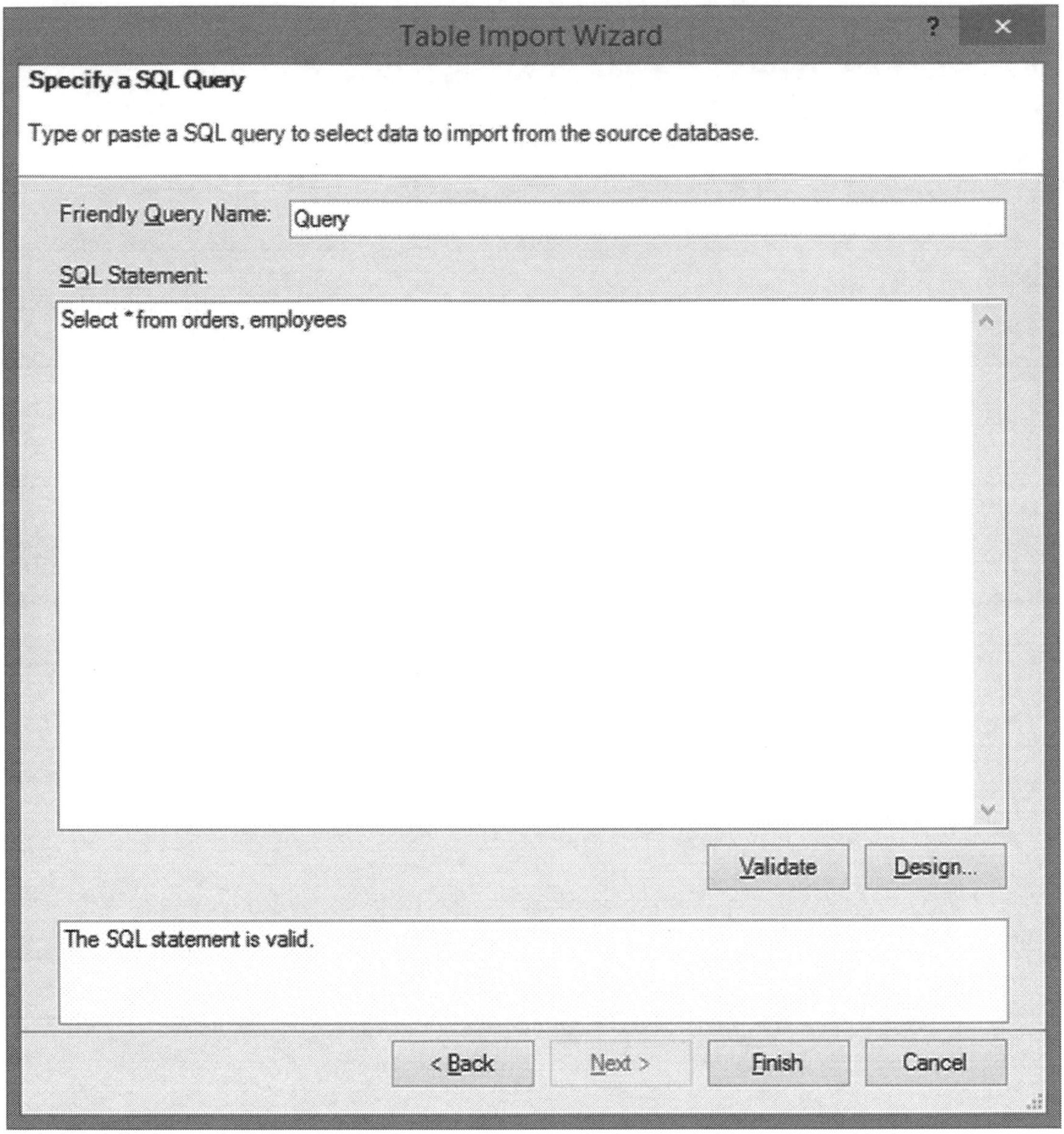

Figure 5-4. *SQL select statement*

9. Click Finish to see the results, which are shown in Figure 5-5. Click Close to access the data.

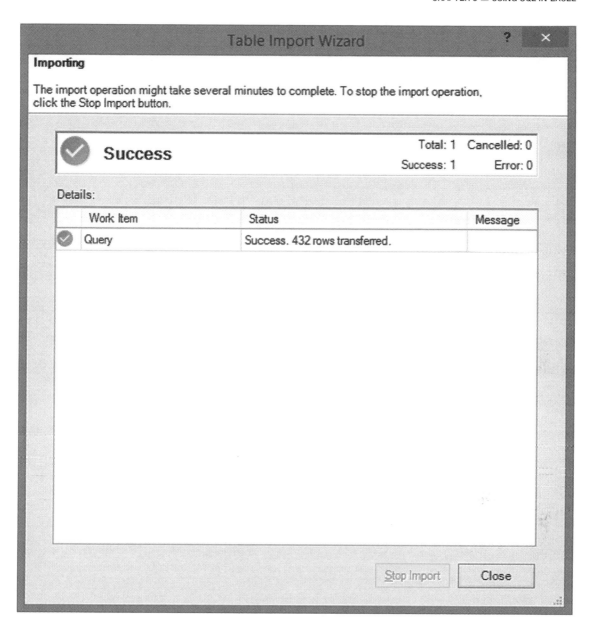

Figure 5-5. *Success screen showing 432 rows imported*

The actual data retrieved after clicking Close is shown in Figure 5-6. Note that 432 rows were imported, because no relationship was specified between the tables, so every row in the first table was paired with every row in the second table. Note that 432 is the product of 9 rows in the employees table and 48 rows in the orders table.

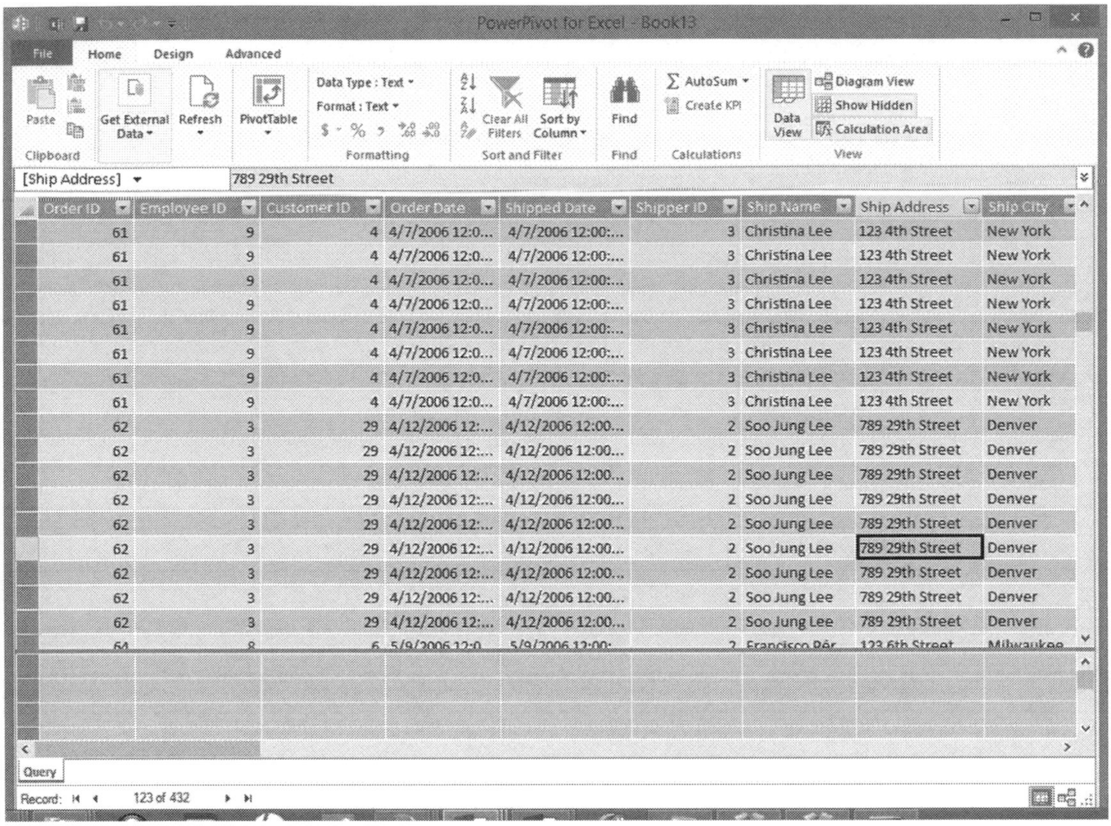

Figure 5-6. *Results table from SQL query*

Specifying a JOIN Condition and Selected Fields

In this example, a join condition will be specified, so that only one order is imported for each employee. This example will show how to import only selected fields. Note that fields with spaces in them must to be enclosed in square brackets. When fields from multiple tables are imported, the field names are specified as tablename.fieldname.

For this example, follow steps 1-6 from the example in the preceding "Importing an External Database" section and then complete the following steps:

1. Enter the SQL statement, as shown in Figure 5-7. Note that the WHERE condition is specified, linking the two tables based on employees.id=orders.[employee id]. The employee last name will be displayed from the employees table. The employee ID will be displayed from both the employees and orders tables, to demonstrate that they are the same.

   ```
   Select employees.id, employees.[last name],orders.[employee id] from employees,
   orders where employees.id=orders.[employee id]
   ```

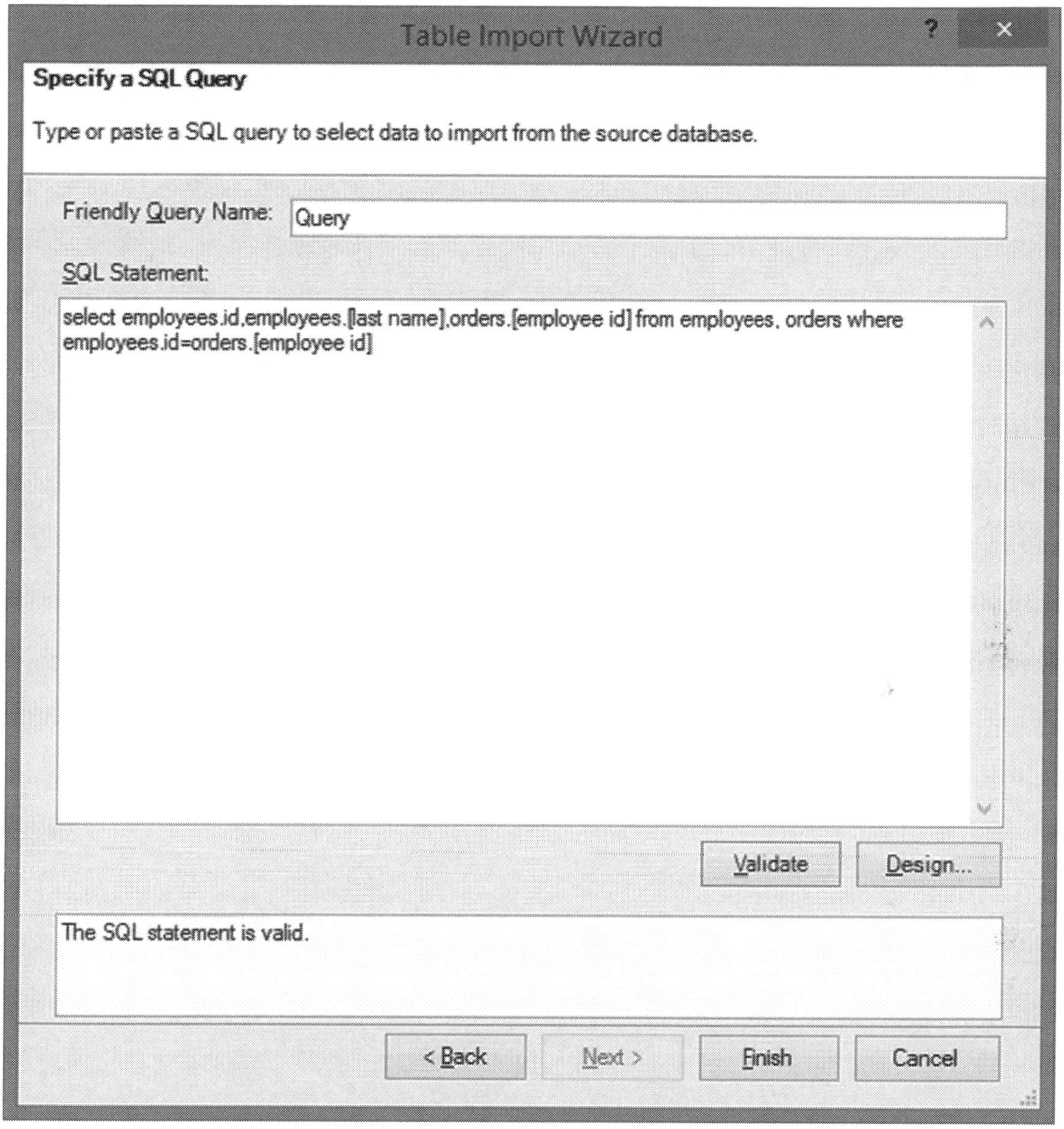

Figure 5-7. *SQL query*

2. Click Validate to ensure that the query is valid, as also shown in Figure 5-7.

3. Now, click Finish. Note that because the condition is specified, only 48 rows (the number of records in the orders table) were imported, as shown in Figure 5-8.

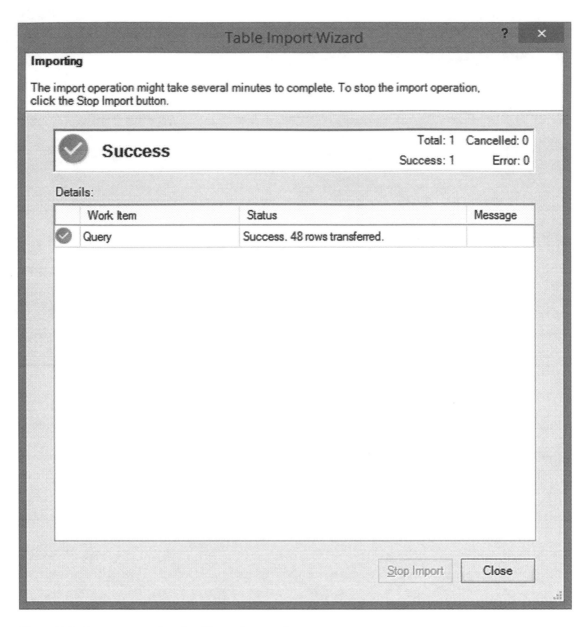

Figure 5-8. *Success screen showing 48 rows imported*

4.   Click Close to complete the procedure. The results are given in Figure 5-9, which shows the employee last name from the employees table and the employee ID from both the employees and orders tables.

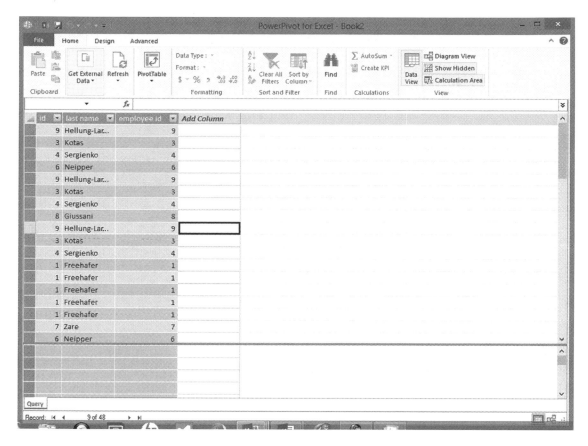

Figure 5-9. *Result table from SQL query*

Using SQL to Extract Summary Statistics

SQL can be used to extract summary statistics from a table or tables using aggregation functions. This example will extract a single number—the sum of unit price times quantity from the orders and orders detail tables.

For this example, follow steps 1-6 from the previous example in the "Importing an External Database" section.

1. Enter the following SQL statement, as shown in Figure 5-10, to extract the sum of price time's quantity for all records in the orders table.

```
Select sum([order details].[unit price] *[order details].quantity) from
orders,[order details]
```

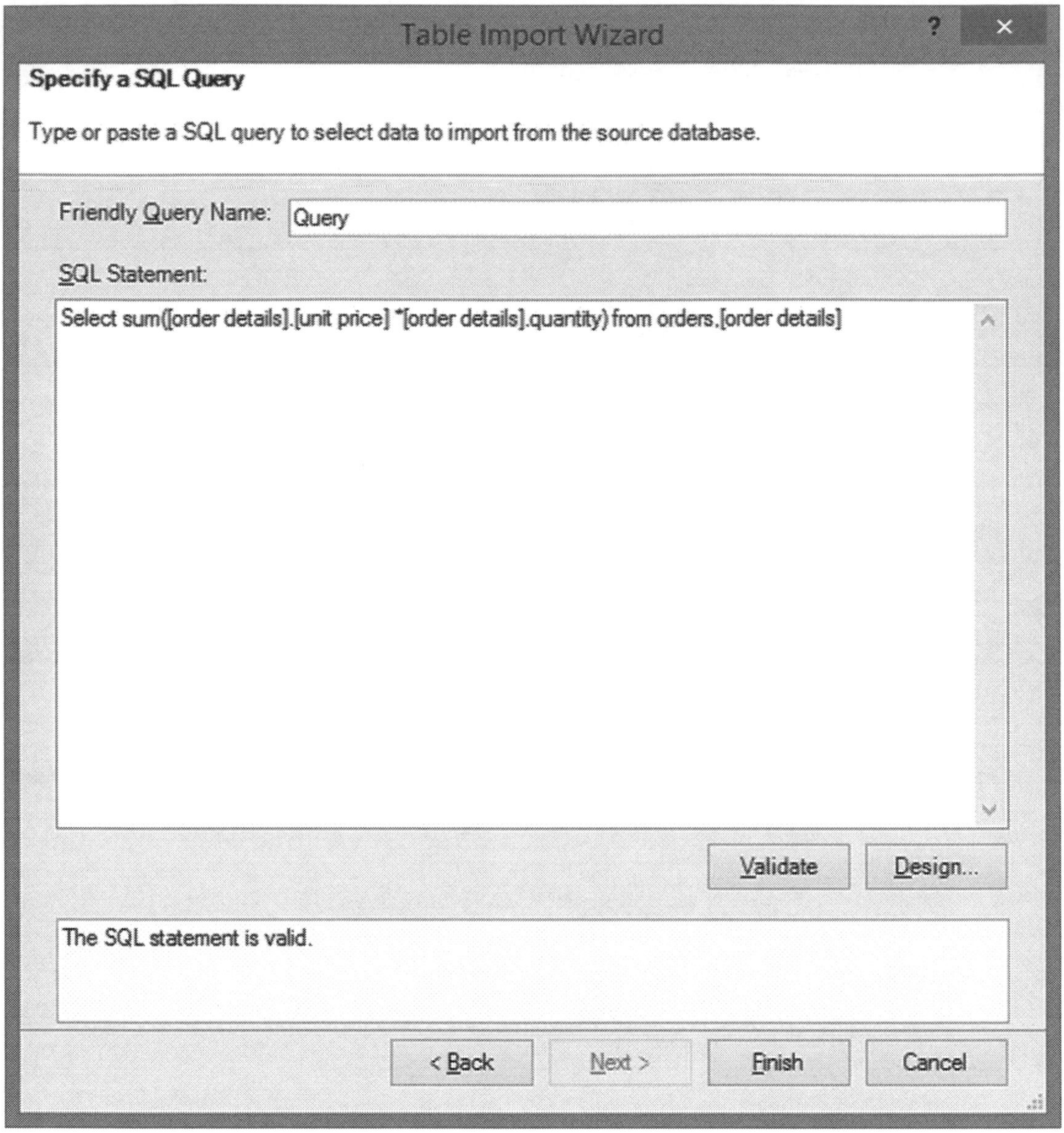

Figure 5-10. *SQL query*

2. Press Enter and wait until the Success screen is shown. Then click Close. The result is shown in Figure 5-11. Notice that the result is a single number, which is the sum of price times quantity for all order detail records.

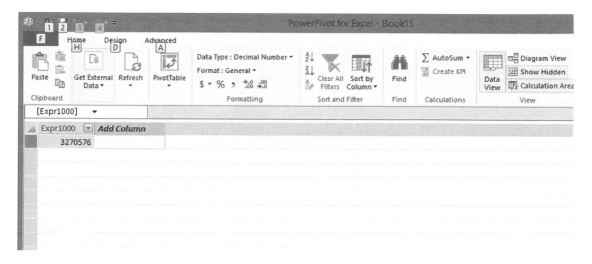

Figure 5-11. *Results is a single number*

Generating a Report of Total Order Value by Employee

In this example, a report will be generated of total order value by employee. To create this report, three tables will be linked: employees, orders, and order details.

For this example, follow steps 1-6 from the previous example in the "Importing an External Database" section.

1. Enter the following SQL statements, as shown in Figure 5-12, to extract the sum of price times quantity for all orders broken down by employee. Click Validate to make sure that the SQL statement is entered correctly.

    ```
    Select employees.[last name], sum([order details].[unit price] * [order details].
    quantity) from employees, orders, [order details] where employees.id=orders.
    [employee id] and orders.[order id]=[order details].[order id] group by
    employees.[last name]
    ```

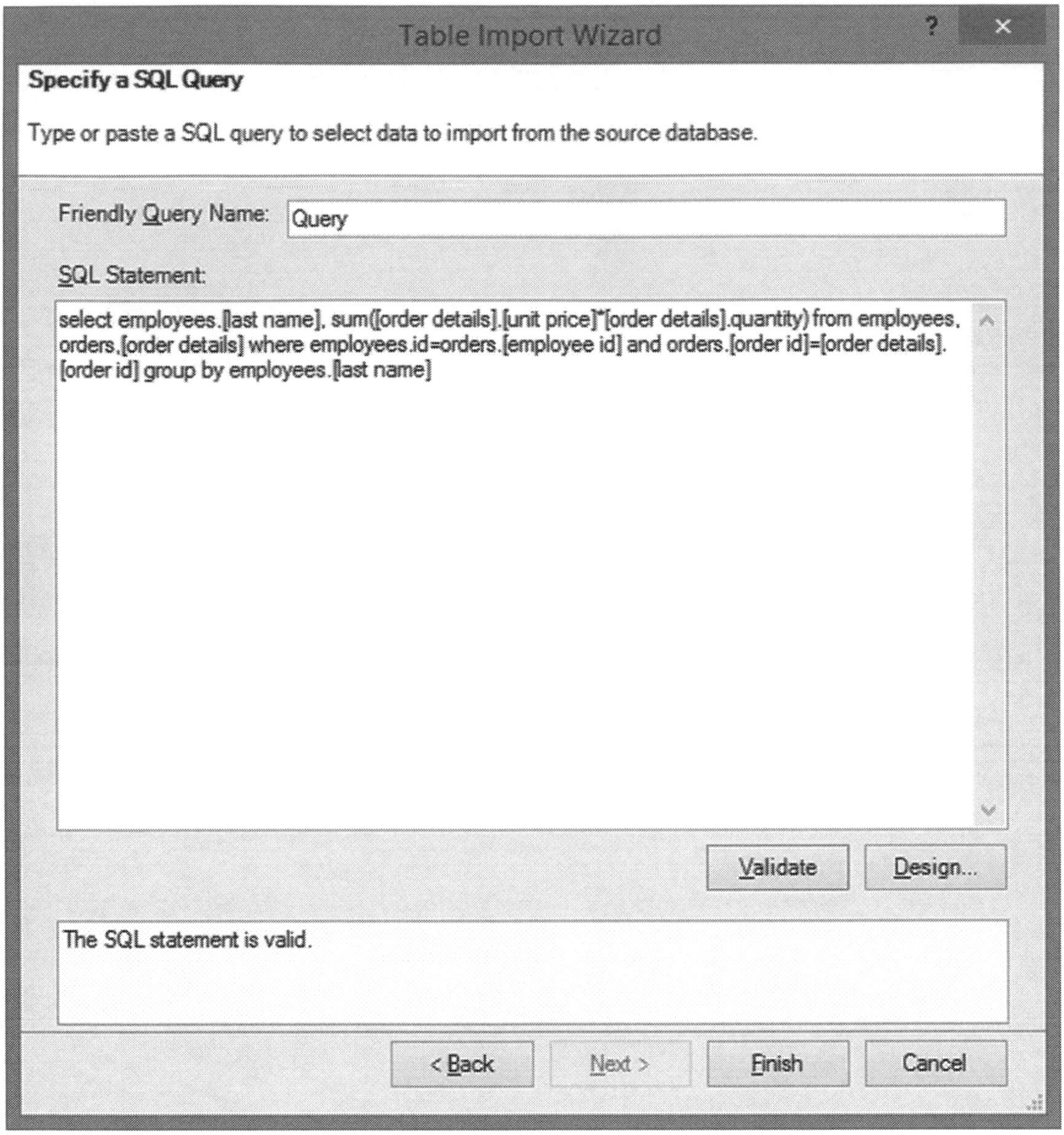

Figure 5-12. *SQL query*

2. Note that two relationships are used to link three tables, based on the relationships shown in Figure 5-3. No fields are displayed from the orders table, but that table is used as a link table. The following are the relationships from Figure 5-3 that are being used in this example. Click Finish to execute the SQL statement.

```
employees.id=orders.[employee id]
orders.[order id]=[order details].[order id]
```

3. This query generates eight rows, as shown in Figure 5-13.

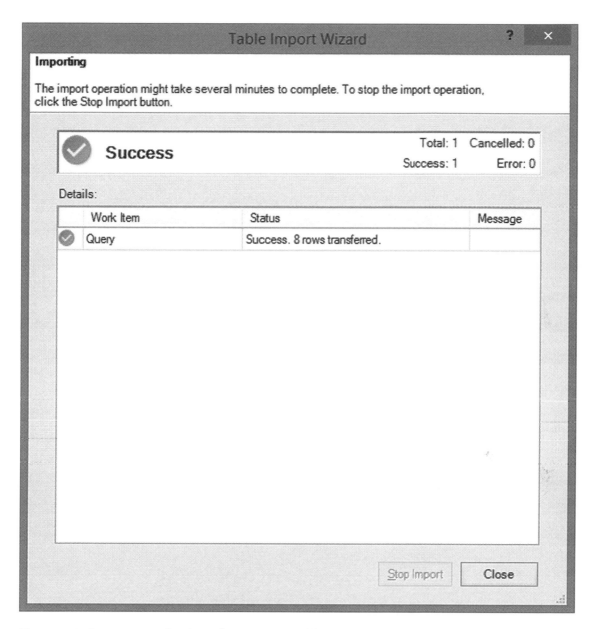

Figure 5-13. *Success screen showing eight rows generated by this query*

4. The actual data generated is shown in Figure 5-14—a listing of the value of orders by employees.

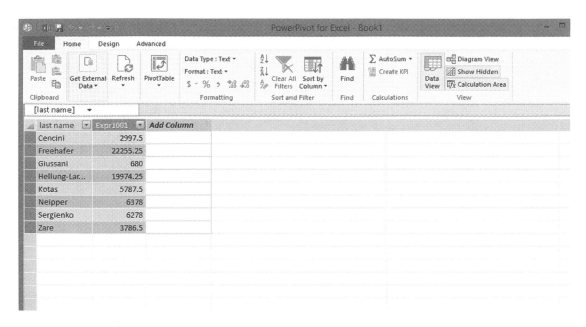

Figure 5-14. *Total value of orders by employee*

Using MSQuery

Another alternative is to use SQL with Microsoft Query. This example will show another way to access the Northwind database used earlier in this chapter. Follow these steps:

1. Click the Data tab to view the ribbon and then click "From Other Sources."

2. Then click the last item on the menu, "From Microsoft Query," as shown in Figure 5-15.

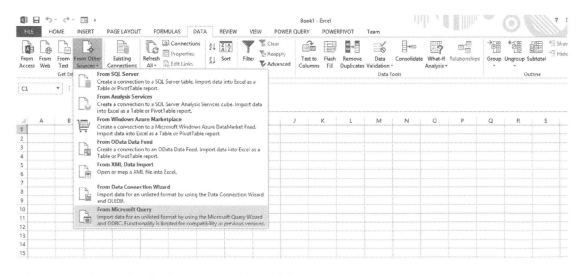

Figure 5-15. *Screen showing how to access Microsoft Query*

3. Select MS Access Database in the Choose Data Source window, as shown in Figure 5-16. Uncheck "Use the Query Wizard to create/edit queries" at the bottom of the window. Then click OK.

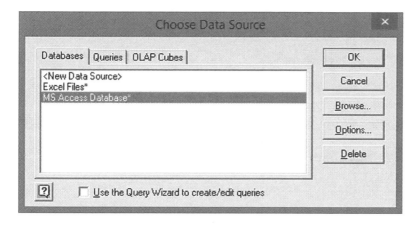

Figure 5-16. *Choose Data Source window*

4. Select Database2, which was downloaded previously, as shown in Figure 5-17, and click OK.

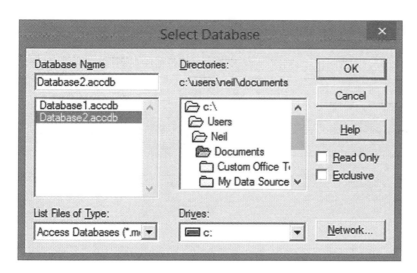

Figure 5-17. *Select Database window*

5. Use the Add Tables window to add the employees, orders, and order detail tables by double-clicking each table, as shown in Figure 5-18.

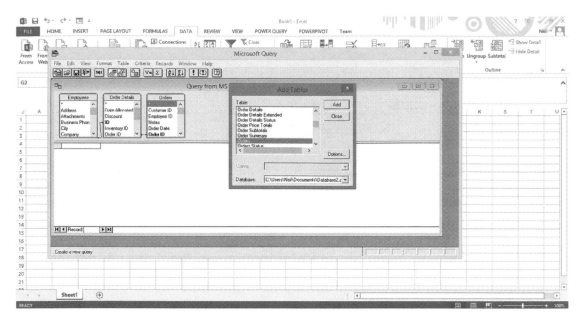

Figure 5-18. *Microsoft Query window to add tables*

6. Click Close and expand the window where the tables are displayed, to see the relationships that have been defined, as shown in Figure 5-19.

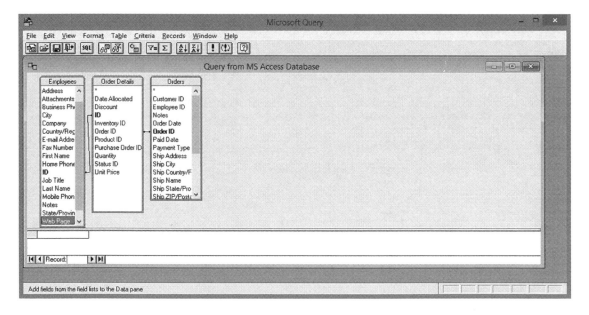

Figure 5-19. *Query screen showing tables and relationships*

7. To enter an SQL query, click the SQL button under the Menu bar and enter the
    SQL query, as shown in Figure 5-20.

```
Select sum([order details].[unit price] *[order details].quantity) from
orders,[order details]
```

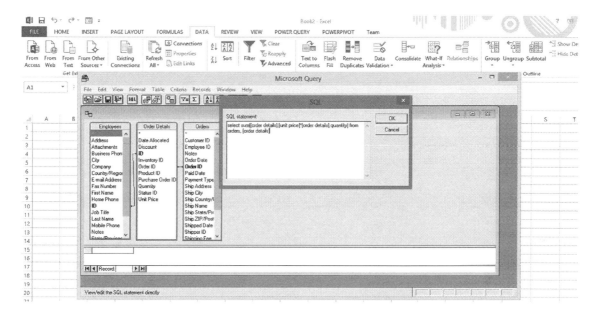

Figure 5-20. *Query screen showing SQL query*

8. Click OK for the prompt "SQL Query can't be represented graphically. Continue
    anyway?", as shown in Figure 5-21.

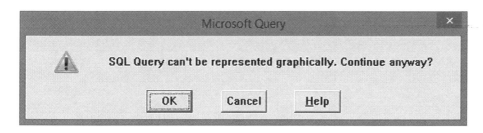

Figure 5-21. *Microsoft Query pop-up window*

The single-number response will be displayed as shown in Figure 5-22.

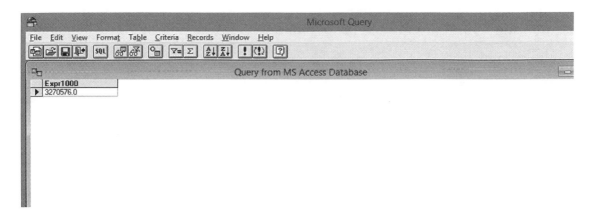

Figure 5-22. *Results of query*

Summary

This chapter has shown several ways in which to use SQL with Excel and PowerPivot to summarize data from a large table or set of tables. It has demonstrated how to join tables based on specified conditions and how to use aggregation to extract summary statistics.

■ ■ ■

Designing Reports with Power View

Power View is a reporting tool that creates its own type of worksheet. For users who are not otherwise proficient in Excel, it is a way of creating a "sandbox" in which to explore a subset of the data without changing it. Power View allows bringing data to life by creating dashboards containing quick and easy visualizations based on PowerPivot models or PivotTables. It is possible to create multiple Power View worksheets based on the same data.

Elements of the Power View Design Screen

The Power View screen consists of the following elements, as shown in Figure 6-1:

1. A design surface on the left

2. A filters area in the middle, where data can be filtered based on field values

3. The Power View Fields pane, where the fields to be included in the report are selected. The top part includes all the available fields, and the bottom part shows the selected fields.

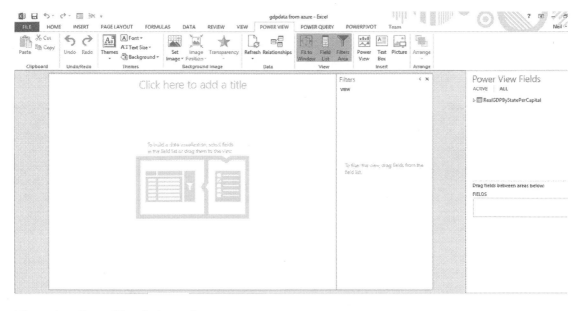

***Figure 6-1.** Power View design surface*

Considerations When Using Power View

Always start with a table view, and then base the chart on the table. It is possible to add multiple tables and/or charts to the design surface. Simply click in a blank area to add a new chart.

Include on the design surface only fields that are necessary for the report. Unless they are relevant to the report, it is generally a good idea to not to include the key values that are used to link tables.

Types of Fields

There are generally two types of fields that are treated very differently.

1. Category or descriptive fields that are nonnumeric

2. Numeric fields that can include calculated fields or measures. The summation symbol is used to indicate a numeric field whose aggregation type can be changed.

Understanding How Data Is Summarized

Perhaps the trickiest part of working with Power View is understanding how data is summarized. By default, numeric fields are summed, even if they are fields in which the sum makes no sense, such as ID number or year. The type of aggregation can be easily changed by clicking the down arrow after the field name in the lower part of the Power View Field pane. The aggregation choices are as follows:

- Do Not Summarize

- Sum

- Average

- Minimum

- Maximum

- Count(Not Blank)

- Count(Distinct)

Note that for data to be plotted on a chart, the field must be summarized using one of the preceding mathematical functions.

A Single Table Example

This first example will show how to use Power View based on a single spreadsheet of the real GDP (gross domestic product) per capita data by state for each year from 1997 to 2011. The instructions to download this data from the Azure Marketplace were covered in Chapter 3. To create the Power View Query, perform the following steps:

1. Open the GDP data from the Azure Spreadsheet, which is shown in Figure 6-2.

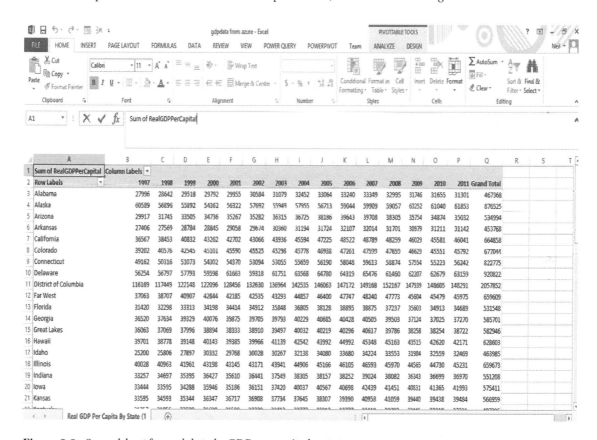

Figure 6-2. *Spreadsheet for real data by GDP per capita by state*

2. Click the Insert tab and select Power View Reports, then wait while the Power View screen loads, as shown in Figure 6-2. If prompted to install SilverLight, click Yes. Note the design surface on the left, the Power View Fields pane on the right, and the Filters pane in the middle.

3. In the Power View Fields pane on the right side of the screen, click the right-facing triangle to the left of RealGDPByStatePerCapita to display the fields. Then drag the year field to the Filters pane, as shown in Figure 6-3.

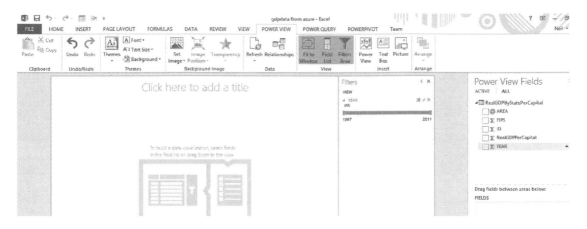

Figure 6-3. *Setting a filter*

4. To display only the most recent year, 2011, click the leftmost icon to the right of Year in the Filters pane to activate the List Filter Mode to see the list of years and select 2011, as shown in Figure 6-4.

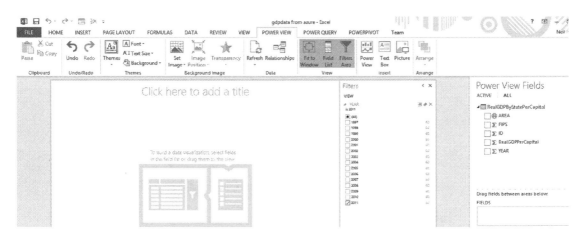

Figure 6-4. *Setting a filter, expanded view*

5. Then, in the Power View Fields pane, click the box in front of Area and RealGDPPerCapita, and a table will be created, as shown in Figure 6-5.

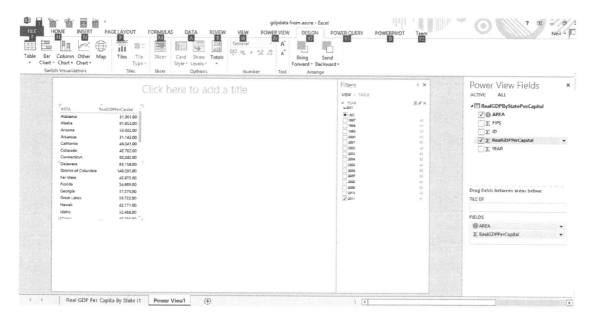

Figure 6-5. *Table showing sum of real GDP per capita*

6. Note that by default, the sum of the RealGDPPerCapita is shown, which is meaningless. If you want to change that setting, at the bottom of the Power View Fields pane, click the down arrow after RealGDPPerCapita and select "Do Not Summarize." However, to plot the charts shown following, it is necessary to leave it set to Sum. The results are shown in Figure 6-6. Note the scrollbar to the right of the table, which allows scrolling through all the states. To expand the table, click it and drag the handles.

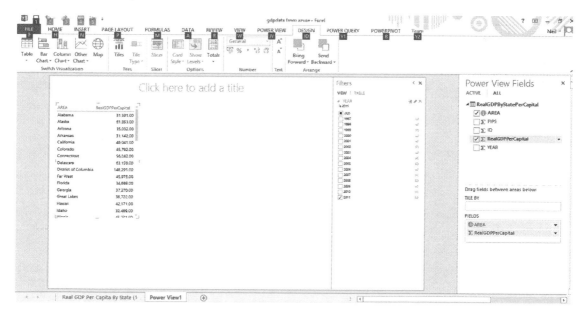

Figure 6-6. *Table showing real GDP per Capita by state*

7. A title can be added by clicking where it says to "Click here to add a title" and entering "Real GDP Per Capita by State for 2011," as shown in Figure 6-7.

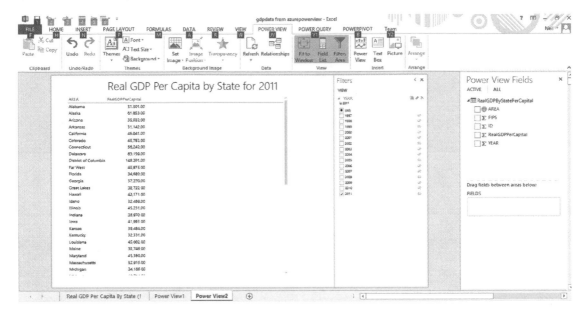

Figure 6-7. *Table with title added*

Viewing the Data in Different Ways

Power View supports multiple formats for viewing data. With the Design tab selected, click the Table icon on the left to see the options: table, matrix, and card. The card view, which creates a card for each state, is shown in Figure 6-8. The matrix view is like a table but allows drilling down. It will be demonstrated in later examples. To go back to the table format, simply click Table under the Table icon.

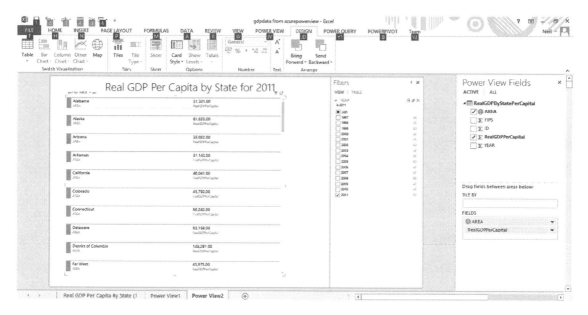

Figure 6-8. *Card view*

Creating a Bar Chart for a Single Year

To create a bar chart showing the real GDP per capita for each state, follow these steps:

1. Click anywhere in the table and select the Design tab. Click Bar Chart. Select Clustered Bar. Because there is a single data source, either clustered or stacked will show the same result.

2. The results will appear as shown in Figure 6-9. A single bar for GDP per capita is shown for each state for the year 2011.

Figure 6-9. *Bar chart*

3. To resize the chart, click it and drag the handles.

Note that you can hover the mouse over any bar in the chart to see the GDP per capita value for that state.

Column Chart

A column chart is a bar chart flipped on its side, as shown in Figure 6-10.

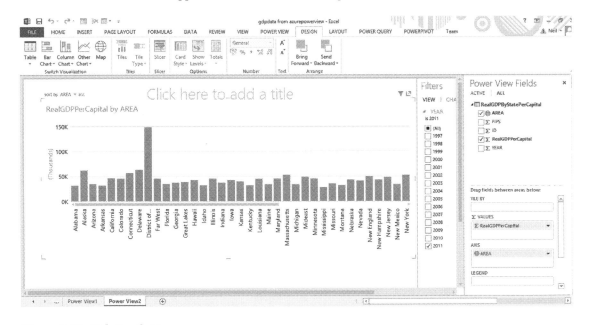

Figure 6-10. *Column chart*

Displaying Multiple Years

If the filter is changed to include multiple years, by clicking the All box at the top of the Years list in the Filters pane, an instance of the state for each year will be generated in the table, as shown in Figure 6-11. It is also necessary to click Year in the Power View Fields list pane, so that the year is displayed.

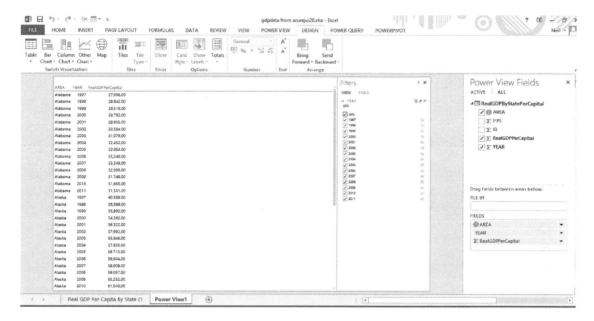

Figure 6-11. *Table for real GDP per capita for multiple years*

If the view is changed to matrix, then it appears as shown in Figure 6-12. Note that it is necessary to tell it not to sum the years, by clicking the arrow after Year in the Fields section of the Power View Fields pane and selecting "Do not summarize."

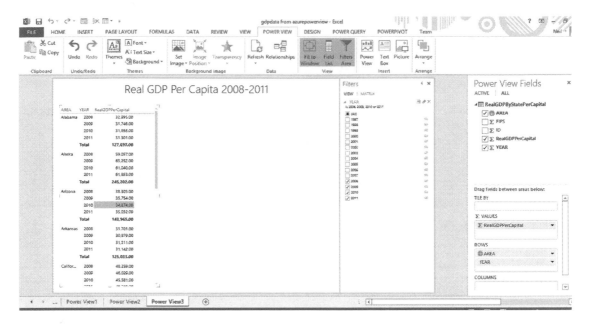

Figure 6-12. *Matrix view of GDP per capita for multiple years*

Adding a Map

To display the data using a map, follow these steps:

1. Click the table to activate the Design tab.

2. Click the Map icon. If a map of the world is displayed, use the Zoom and Pan icons at the upper right to display only the desired area of the map, as shown in Figure 6-13. Hover the mouse over a bubble to see the actual number associated with it.

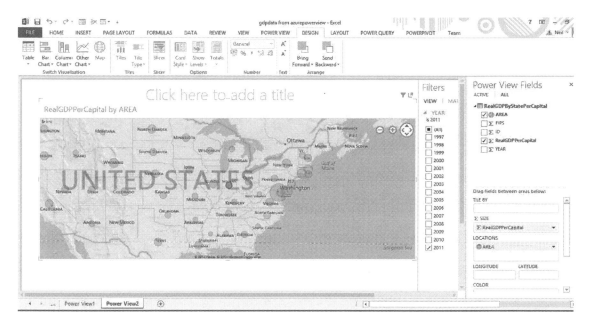

Figure 6-13. *Map view showing GDP per capita by state*

Note that bubbles are displayed for each state proportional to the GDP per capita for that state. In the Filters pane, individual or multiple years can be selected to see the data for those years.

Using Tiles

Another way of viewing the data is by using tiles. Simply select a table and click the Tiles icon on the Design toolbar to see a display, as shown in Figure 6-14. The default layout has a tab strip at the top of the display that allows clicking each state to see the values for that state.

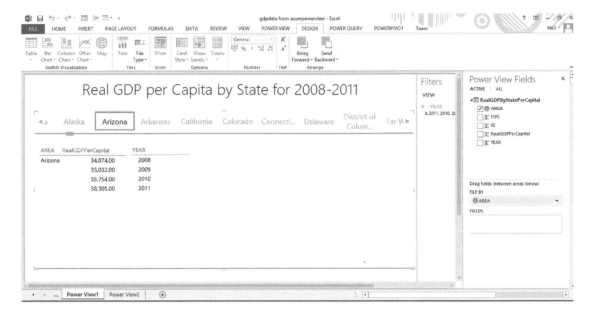

Figure 6-14. *Tile format*

An alternative is the tile flow format with the tiles at the bottom as shown in Figure 6-15. These views can be toggled by clicking on the Tile Type icon on the Design toolbar.

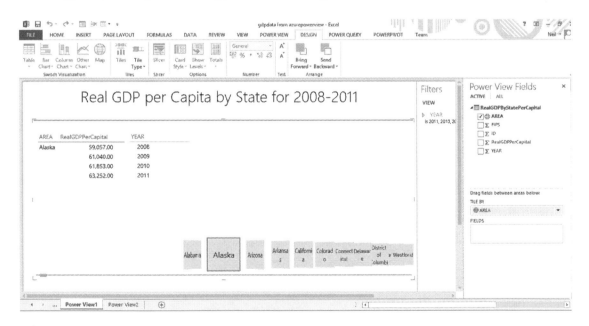

Figure 6-15. *Tile Flow format*

Relational Example

For this example, Access database2 (the Northwind Database) will be used. Some of the imported tables are shown in Figure 6-16. This database can be downloaded from the Apress web site.

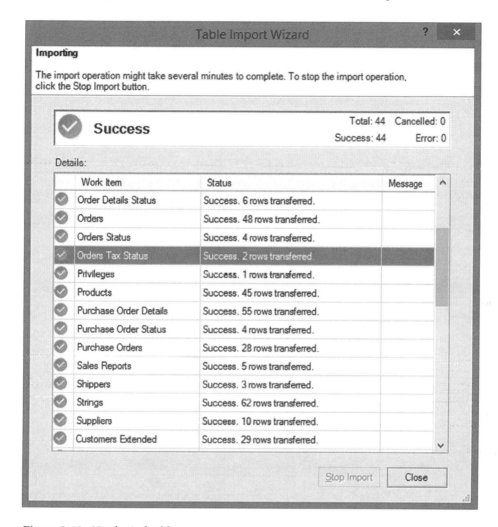

Figure 6-16. *Northwind tables*

Follow the steps described in Chapter 4 to import Access data.

1. Click the PowerPivot tab to open the ribbon.

2. Click the Manage button at the top-left end of the ribbon.

3. Once the PowerPivot window is open, you can load data by clicking *From Database* in the Get External Data group. This provides a choice of database sources. For this example, *From Access* will be selected.

4. In the Table Import Wizard dialog, click the Browse button to find the Access file you want to import. For this example, use `Database2.accdb`. This file is available from the Apress web site.

5. Click *Test Connection*. If the test is successful, click Next.

6. PowerPivot opens the Table Import Wizard to take you through the process of loading data. Choose *Select from a list of tables and views to choose the data you want to import*. Click Next.

7. Click the top-left box to select all tables. Note that in the lower right corner of the dialog, there is an option to *Preview & Filter*. This option can be used to select a subset of data from very large datasets. In this example, all rows in all tables will be imported. Then click Finish to complete the import.

8. The tables imported are shown in Figure 6-16.

The relationships between the tables are shown in Figure 6-17.

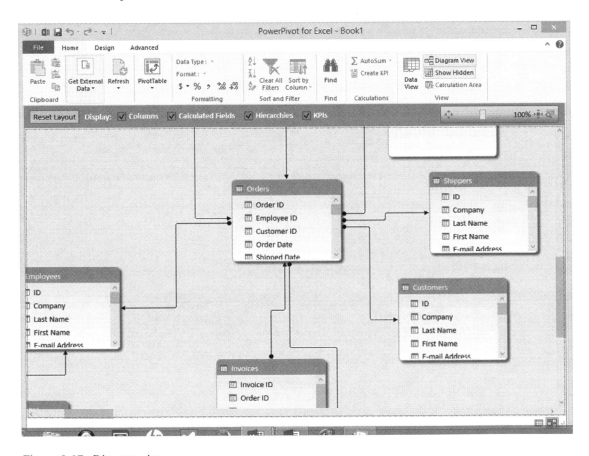

Figure 6-17. *Diagram view*

This example will use the relation between customer ID in the orders table and the ID field in the customers table.

Another view of the relationships is shown in Figure 6-18, which is accessed by clicking the Relationships icon on the Data tab.

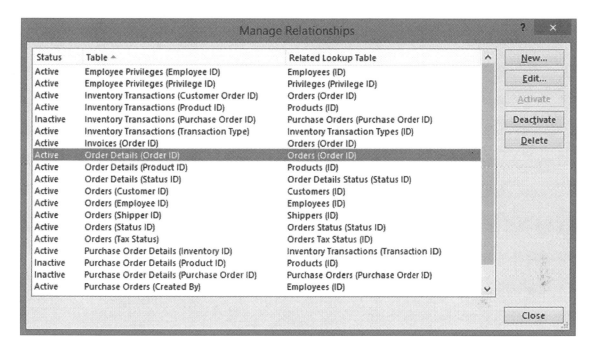

Figure 6-18. *Relationships*

To create a Power View report, follow these steps:

1. Click Power View Reports on the Excel Insert tab.

2. First create a table by selecting fields from the Power View Fields tab on the right side of the screen.

3. From the customers table, select the company, first name, and job title fields, as shown in Figure 6-19.

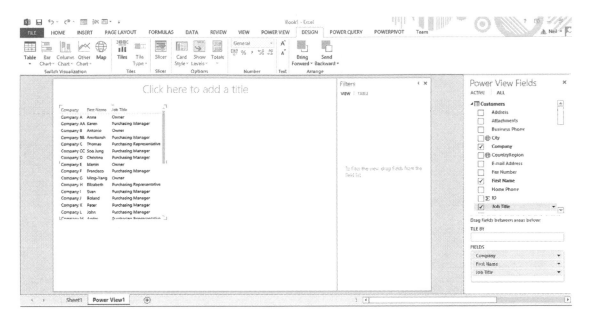

Figure 6-19. *Table showing company, first name, and job title*

4. Next, select Price Total from the Order Price Totals table. Doing this depends on the relationship between the customers to orders table to the order price totals table. The results are shown in Figure 6-20.

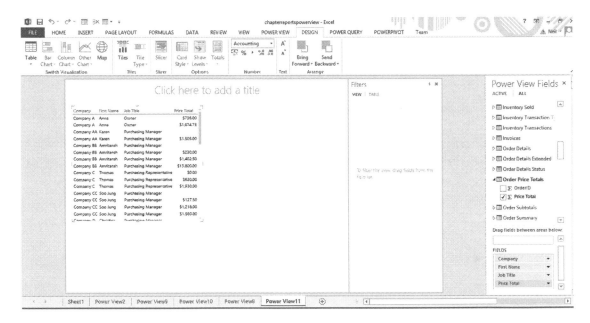

Figure 6-20. *Table showing order totals*

5. Note that for companies with multiple orders, there are multiple rows shown in the table. A matrix view, shown in Figure 6-21, makes this more obvious.

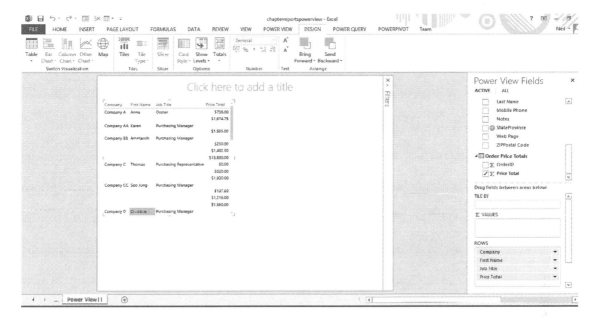

Figure 6-21. *Matrix view*

Customer and City Example

This example will show customers by city. The objective is to show the value of orders from each city. Follow these steps:

1. Click Power View Reports on the Excel Insert tab.

2. Select company and city from the Customers table, as shown in Figure 6-22. Adjust the width of the company column in the table, if necessary, by selecting the line between columns in the title bar and dragging.

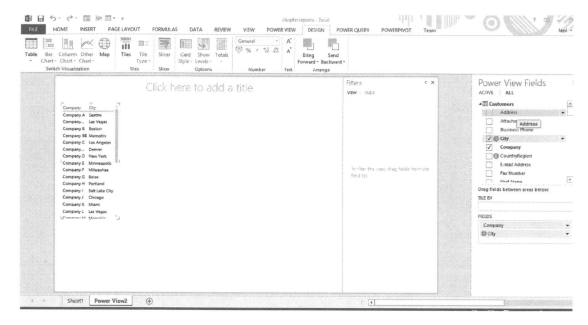

Figure 6-22. *Company and city table*

3. Select the price total field from the order price totals table. Note that a prompt appears to create a relation. Because no relation is created, the total of all orders is shown, as in Figure 6-23.

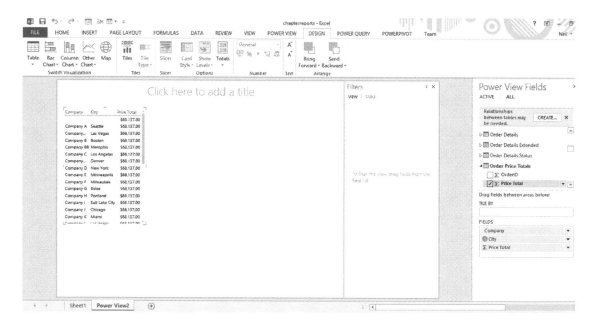

Figure 6-23. *Table showing company, city, and order price totals*

4. Create the relationship between the orders table and the order price totals table based on the order ID, as shown in Figure 6-24, and click OK.

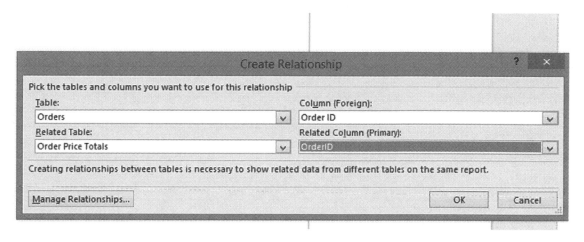

Figure 6-24. *Creating relationship between the orders and order price totals tables*

5. Next, click the arrow after Price Total in the Fields list and select "Do Not Summarize," as shown in Figure 6-25. Note that the value of each order is now shown, instead of the total of all orders.

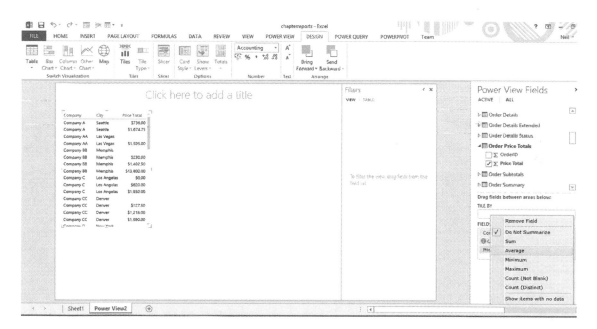

Figure 6-25. *Table showing individual order totals*

6. Selecting the matrix view by clicking Table on the Design tab and selecting Matrix and clicking "Fit to Window" will result in the display shown in Figure 6-26. Note that a title has been entered. The view can be scrolled using the scrollbars on the right.

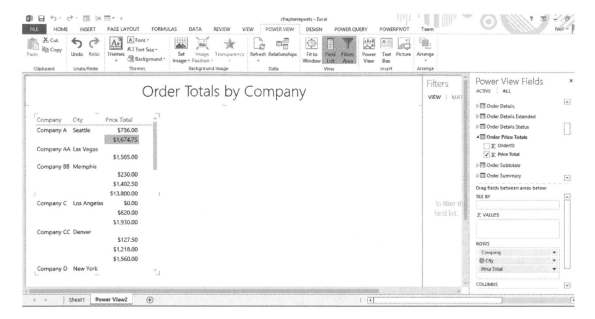

Figure 6-26. *Matrix view*

7. Clicking the pop-out icon at the upper right of the table display will result in the view shown in Figure 6-27.

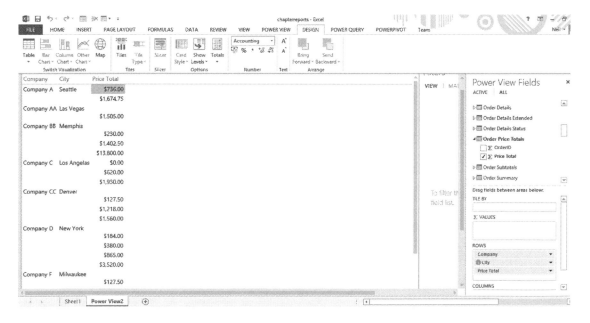

Figure 6-27. *Pop-out view of the matrix*

8.   To filter out records that do not have an order, drag the Price Total field to the
     Filters pane and drag the left bar to the right to some arbitrary small number
     greater than zero, as shown in Figure 6-28.

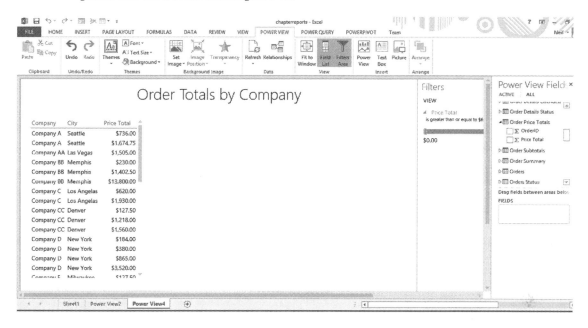

Figure 6-28. *Filtering out companies with no orders*

Or click on the Price Total field name and set the filter as greater than or equal to 1 and click Apply Filter,
as shown in Figure 6-29.

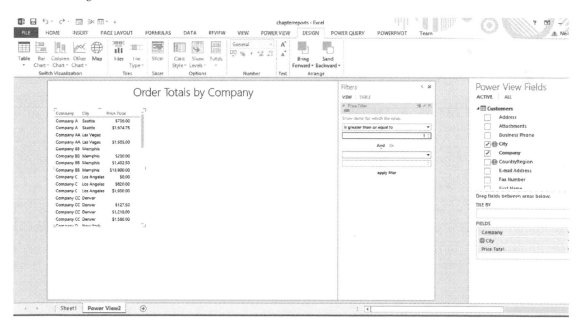

Figure 6-29. *Another way to filter out companies with no orders*

Showing Orders by Employee

The next example will show number of orders by employee, by taking the following steps:

1. Create a new Power View sheet by clicking Power View on the Power View tab.

2. Enter the title "Orders by Employee."

3. In the Power View Fields pane, select the Last Name field from the Employees table.

Then select the Order ID field from the Orders table. The results are shown in Figure 6-30. Note that by default, it sums the Order IDs, which is a meaningless number.

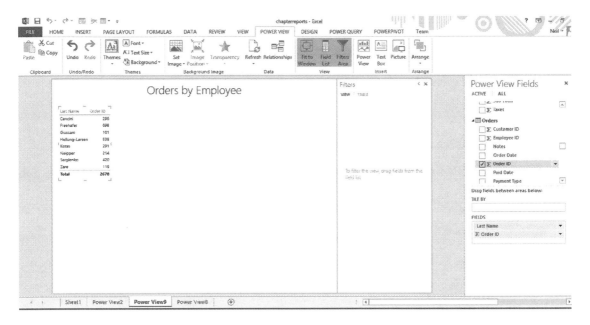

Figure 6-30. *Table showing employees and orders*

4. In the Fields area of the Power View Fields pane, click the arrow after Order ID and select *count (non blank)*. The results are shown in Figure 6-31. Note that a count of the orders is now shown in the table.

Figure 6-31. *Table showing employees and number of orders per employee*

5. To create a chart of the data, right-click the table and select Copy. Click in the blank area next to the table, right-click, and select Paste to get another copy of the table, as shown in Figure 6-32.

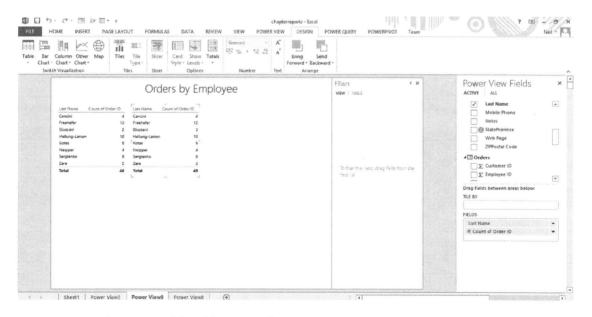

Figure 6-32. *Making a copy of the table prior to plotting*

6. To plot the chart, select the rightmost table that was just pasted, click the Bar
    Chart icon on the Design tab, and select Stacked Bar to get a bar chart, as shown
    in Figure 6-33.

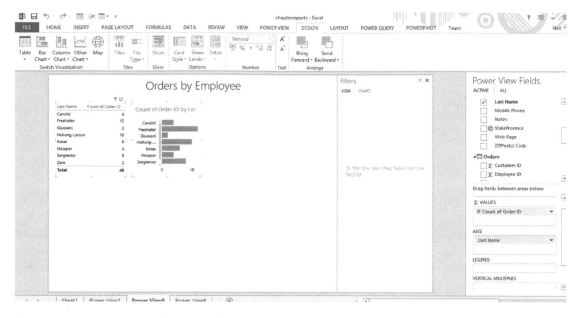

Figure 6-33. *Bar chart of orders by employee*

Aggregating Orders by Product

This example will show the number of orders by product. Follow these steps:

1. Click Power View Reports on the Excel Insert tab.

2. Select the Product Name field in the products table in the Power View Fields
    pane, as shown in Figure 6-34.

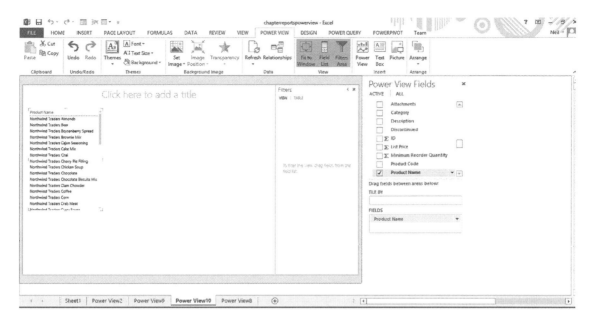

Figure 6-34. *Product list*

3. Next, select the Quantity field in the Order Details Table, as shown in Figure 6-35. Note that the sum of the quantity is shown.

Figure 6-35. *Quantity of products ordered*

4. Click anywhere in the table and use the handles to expand it, as shown in Figure 6-36.

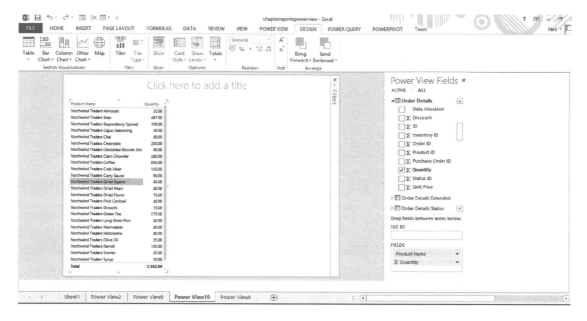

Figure 6-36. *Expanded view of table*

5. To create a chart, right-click the table and select copy. Click to the right of the table on the design surface and select Paste. Then, on the Design tab, select Bar Chart and Stacked Bar. At the top of the design screen, enter the title "Product Quantity Sold." The result is shown in Figure 6-37.

Figure 6-37. *Bar chart of product quantity sold*

Note that in the bar chart, only the first nine characters of the name are shown. It is possible to hover the mouse pointer over any bar in the bar chart to see the full product name and quantity sold. To display more characters, click the chart window to select it, and drag the handles to expand the size, as shown in Figure 6-38.

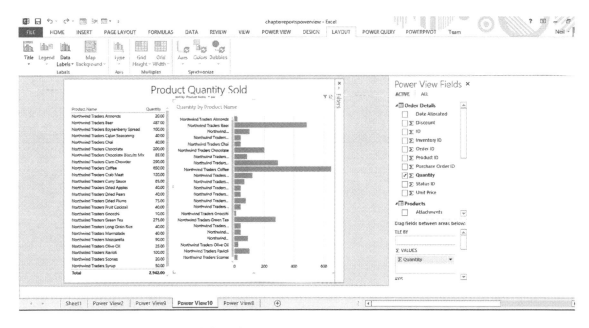

Figure 6-38. *Bar chart with expanded product name*

Summary

This chapter has just scratched the surface of showing how to use Power View to easily generate data tables and charts to bring data to life. It has covered how to analyze sales by city, by employee, and product. Creating simple maps has also been demonstrated. Chapter 9 will show how to create more sophisticated maps, using Power Map.

CHAPTER 7

■ ■ ■

Calculating with Data Analysis Expressions (DAX)

This chapter covers calculations with Data Analysis Expressions (DAX) and measuring performance with Key Performance Indicators (KPIs). It will focus on some practical examples of the use of DAX and KPIs.

Understanding Data Analysis Expressions

As explained in Chapter 4, Data Analysis Expressions (DAX) is a formula language used to create calculated columns and fields based on the tabular data model of PowerPivot. DAX formulas differ from regular Excel formulas, which are cell-based, in that DAX formulas apply to all rows in the specified columns. DAX formulas are used in the following two contexts:

1. *Calculated columns.* Calculated columns can be added to an existing PowerPivot table. When a column contains a formula, the value is calculated for each row. To create a formula, click any cell in a new column and press Enter to start entering a formula that is based on column references. Column names can be referenced by pointing to them with the mouse or by entering the names enclosed in square brackets. Columns from other worksheets can be referenced by entering the worksheet name before the column name. If the worksheet name contains a space, it can be enclosed in single quotes. Up to 64 levels of functions can be nested in a DAX expression.

2. *Calculated fields or measures.* These are placed in the calculation area at the bottom of the PowerPivot window. Calculated fields often include aggregation functions, such as sum or average, which by default reference the entire column. DAX functions are very similar to Excel functions, but DAX functions are column-oriented. All available DAX functions can be viewed by clicking the fx icon on the Design tab of the PowerPivot window. When a calculated field is created, the formula is preceded by an identifier, which is like a variable name and can be used to reference the calculated field.

■ **Caution**   When using DAX, it is best to avoid using the same name for a calculated field and a calculated column. To further avoid ambiguity, it is best when, referencing a column, to use the fully qualified column name, which includes the name of the worksheet.

DAX Operators

DAX uses the following:

the standard arithmetic operators

+	Addition
-	Subtraction
*	Multiplication
/	Division
^	Exponentiation

the comparison operators

=	Equal
>	Greater than
<	Less than
>=	Greater than or equal to
<=	Less than or equal to
<>	Not equal to

the text concatenation operator

| & | Concatenation |

and the logical operators

| && | And |
| \|\| | OR |

Summary of Key DAX Functions Used in This Chapter

SUM: A simple sum, such as in Excel

SUMX: Iterates through one row at a time in order to do calculations

CALCULATE: Allows calculating based on a filter condition

LEFT: Returns the specified number of characters from the start of the named text string

Updating Formula Results

There are two ways to update the results of formulas.

1. Refreshing data involves updating the data in the underlying data source, such as SQL Server, MySQL, or Access.

2. Recalculating involves updating the results of formulas based on changes to the formulas.

ANALYZING SALES DATA

This chapter will continue the example used at the end of Chapter 4—the Contoso database available for download from Tinyurl.com/PowerPivotSamples. Note that the URL is case-sensitive. Once the data is downloaded, open the PowerPivotTutorialSamples spreadsheet.

One way of thinking about this example is to use a star model architecture that includes a fact table containing the numbers that have to be aggregated, surrounded by dimension tables, such as products and stores. In this example, the dboFactSales table is the fact table, as shown in Figure 7-1. To create this example, follow these steps:

1. Click Manage on the PowerPivot tab and then click on Diagram View to see the tables in Diagram View as shown in Figure 7-1.

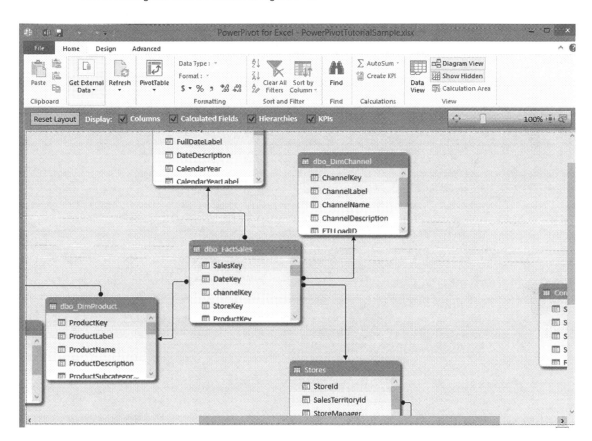

Figure 7-1. *Diagram View*

2. Click Data View and then click the dbo_FactSales tab at the bottom of the window to view the dbo_FactSales tab. Scroll all the way to the right and notice the final column, TotalProfit, which is a DAX calculated field based on TotalSales minus TotalCost, as shown in Figure 7-2. Click any cell in the column to see the formula displayed just below the ribbon.

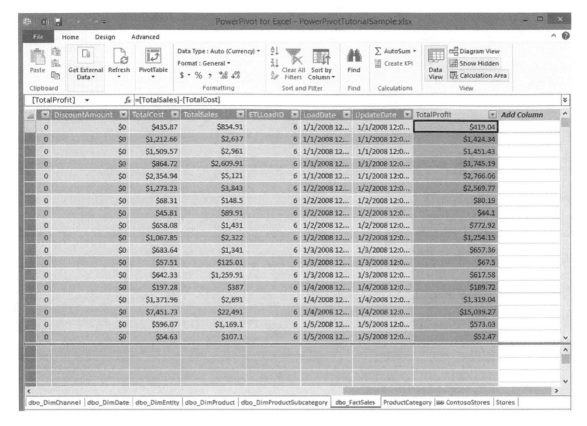

Figure 7-2. *Calculated column*

Creating Measures or Calculated Fields

This section shows how to create measures or calculated fields based on the data in the tables.

1. To add a calculated field or measure, go to the first cell below the data grid at the bottom of the TotalProfit column and select the cell. Double-click the AutoSum icon on the tab to get the sum. If the calculation area or measure grid at the bottom of the data grid is not visible, click the Calculation Area icon at the right end of the tab.

2. Next, select the cell below the sum cell just created, click the down arrow after the AutoSum icon, and from the drop-down, select average, as shown in Figure 7-3. It may be necessary to expand the column to see the totals. Do that by clicking the bar separating the column headings, and when a double arrow appears, drag to the right. Note that an identifier "Sum of Total Profits" and "Average of Total Profits" is created. This identifier acts as both a label and a variable name used to reference the calculated field.

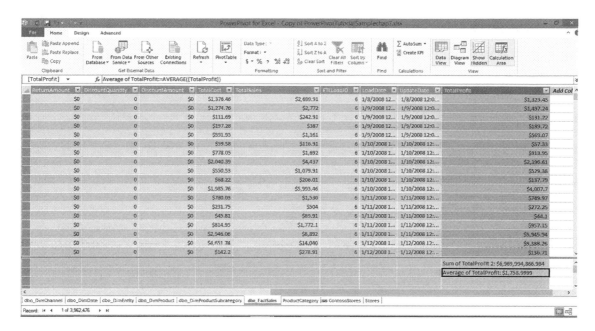

Figure 7-3. *Calculated fields*

3. Follow the same steps with the Total Sales column to add the sum and average, as shown in Figure 7-4.

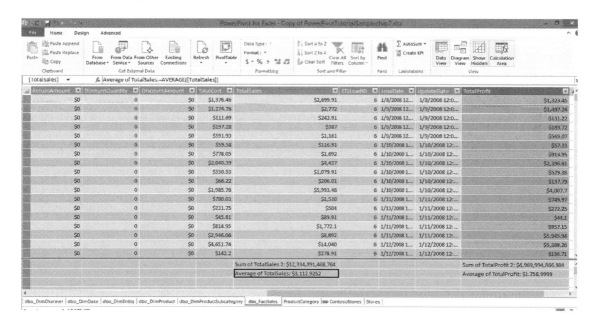

Figure 7-4. *Additional calculated fields*

Analyzing Profitability

This example will show how to insert a new column to analyze the profitability of each transaction.

1. Add a calculated column for profitability or profit divided by sales by clicking anywhere in the rightmost column named "Add Column" and pressing "=". Then click the TotalProfit column, press /, and click the TotalSales column to define the formula and then press Enter. The result is shown in Figure 7-5.

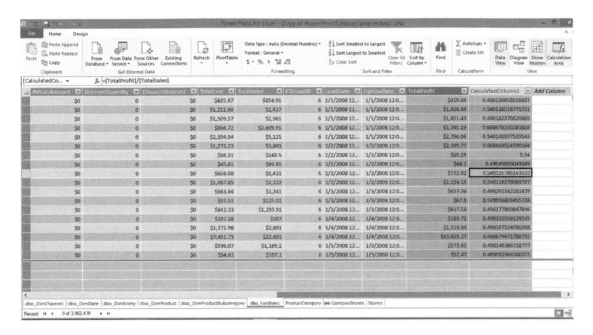

Figure 7-5. *Calculated field for profit/sales*

2. To format the column to display percentages, select the new column and then click the down arrow after Format on the Home tab and select Percentage. The result is shown in Figure 7-6.

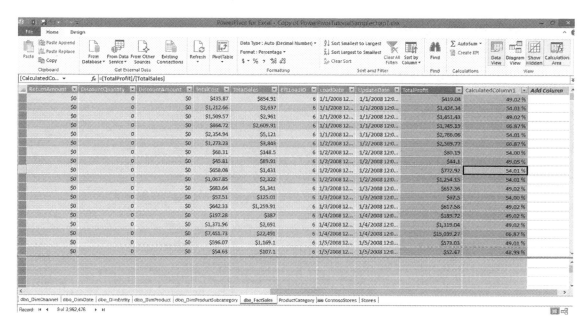

Figure 7-6. Formatting as percentage

3. To rename the column, right-click the column heading, select Rename Column, and enter Profit/Sales, as shown in Figure 7-7.

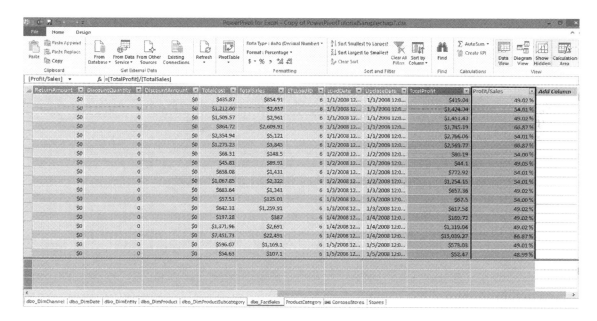

Figure 7-7. Renaming a calculated column

4. To create a calculated field that is the average of all the profit/sales, go down to the calculation area below the data area. Select the cell at the bottom of the Profit/Sales column and then click the down arrow after the AutoSum icon on the ribbon and select average. A calculated field will be created, as shown in Figure 7-8. Expand the column as necessary to display the full value.

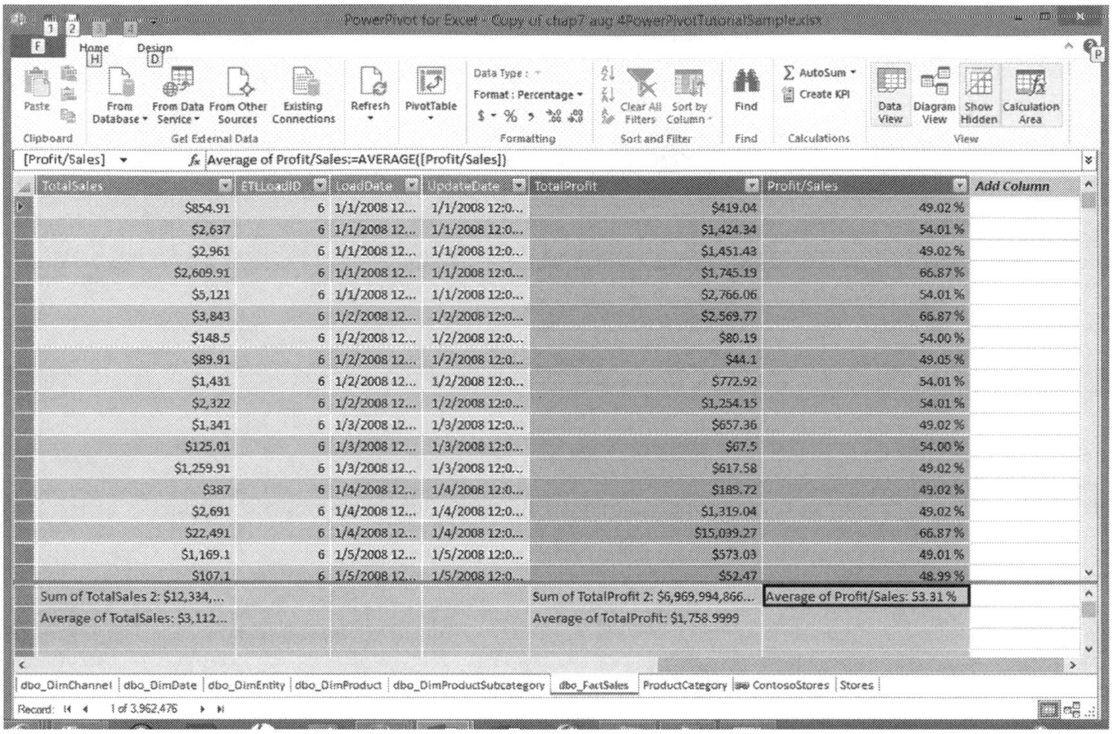

Figure 7-8. *Average of Profit/Sales*

5. To add calculated fields for minimum and maximum profit/sales, select the cell in the calculation area just below the one where the average is. Click the arrow after AutoSum on the ribbon, select maximum, and then repeat and select minimum. Calculated fields for average minimum and maximum will be created, as shown in Figure 7-9.

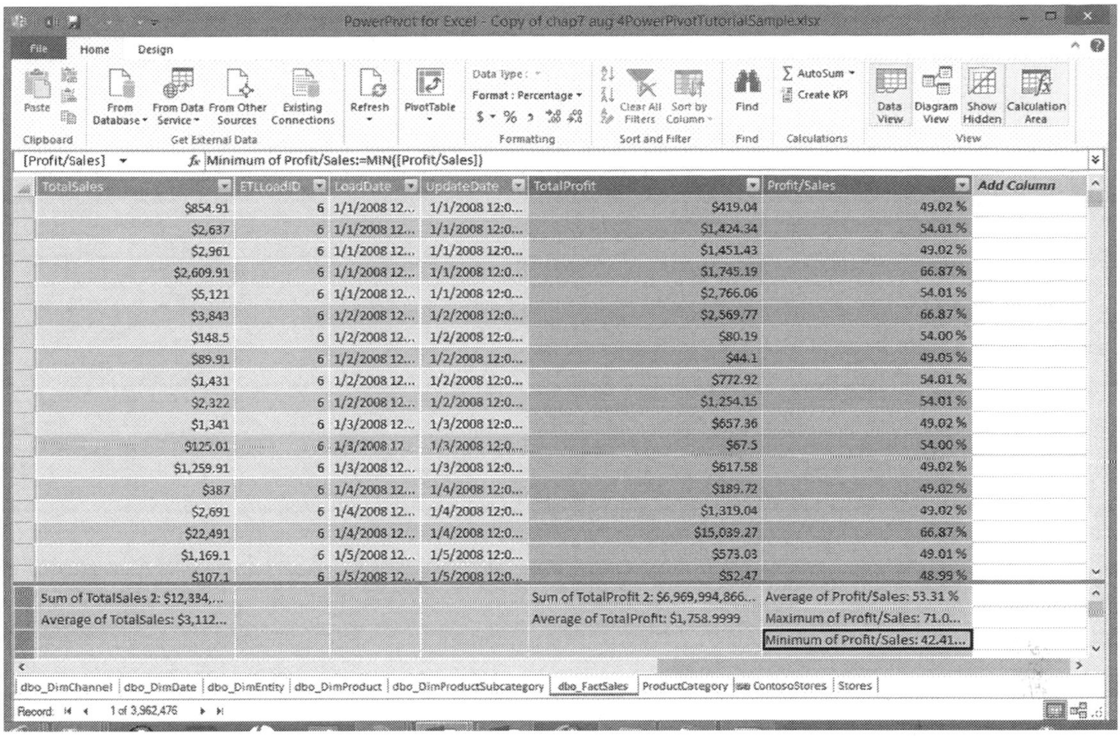

Figure 7-9. *Adding calculated fields for minimum and maximum profit/sales*

Using the SUMX Function

The SUM function can be used to sum a single column. By contrast, SUMX iterates through each column and performs a calculation. So, for instance, SUMX could be used to sum the product of price time's quantity for each row. To do so, follow these steps:

1. Select the next cell down in the first column of the calculation area.

2. Enter the following formula to test SUMX and format it as currency, as shown in Figure 7-10:

```
testsumx:=SUMX(dbo_FactSales,dbo_FactSales[UnitPrice]*
dbo_FactSales[SalesQuantity])
```

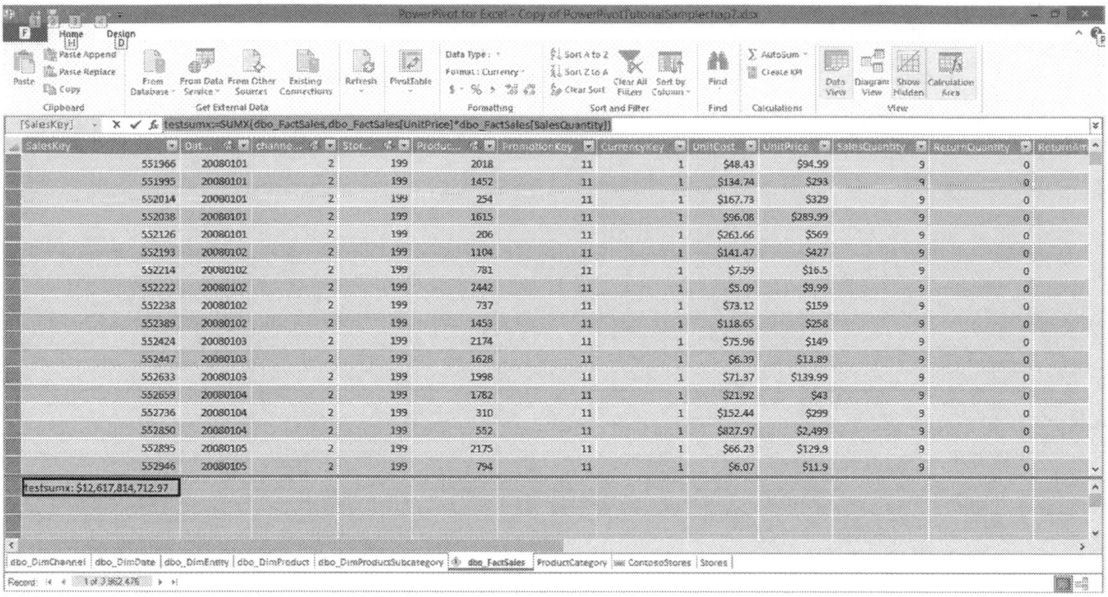

Figure 7-10. *Using the SUMX function*

Using the CALCULATE Function

The CALCULATE() function is used to calculate an expression based on a filter. The following example calculates total sales through the store channel. Follow these steps:

1. Select the top leftmost cell in the Calculation area.

2. Enter the formula, as shown in Figure 7-11. The DAX formula is

```
StoreSales:=CALCULATE(SUM(dbo_FactSales[TotalSales]),
dbo_DimChannel[ChannelName]="Store")
```

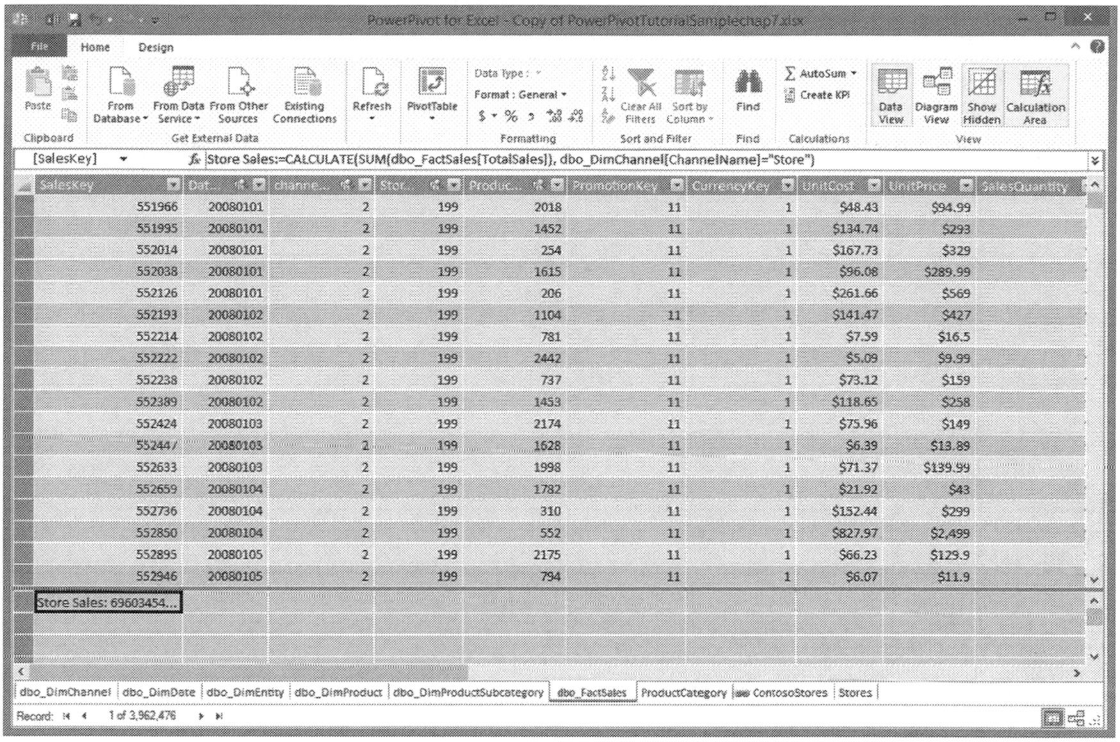

Figure 7-11. *Using the CALCULATE function to show total store sales*

Note that the formula starts with a label, followed by a colon. StoreSales is both the label and identifier for this calculated field. CALCULATE will then sum the TotalSales field from the dbo_FactSales table, in which the channel name is equal to store. When typing a function name or field name, Intellisense pops up a list of what it thinks you want to enter. Highlight the desired value and press Tab to select.

1. Note that the total sales number is not formatted. This can be corrected by selecting the field and clicking the down arrow after the Format icon on the ribbon and selecting currency. The column also needs to be expanded, which can be achieved by clicking the bar between column headings and dragging. The result is shown in Figure 7-12.

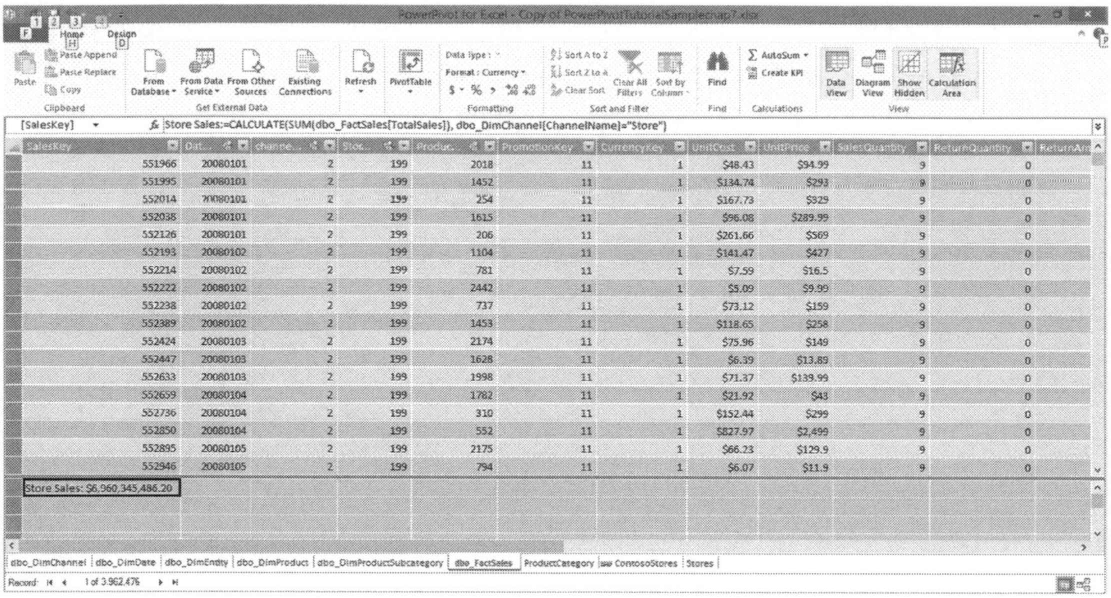

Figure 7-12. *Formatting as currency*

Calculating the Store Sales for 2009

Calculated fields can be based on other calculated fields. The store sales for 2009 can be calculated based on the total StoreSales calculated field. Follow these steps:

1. Select the next cell in the leftmost calculation area.

2. Enter the following formula:

```
StoreSales2009:=CALCULATE([StoreSales],LEFT(dbo_DimDate[Datekey],4)="2009")
```

The LEFT function is used to extract the year from the Datekey text string. The result is shown in Figure 7-13.

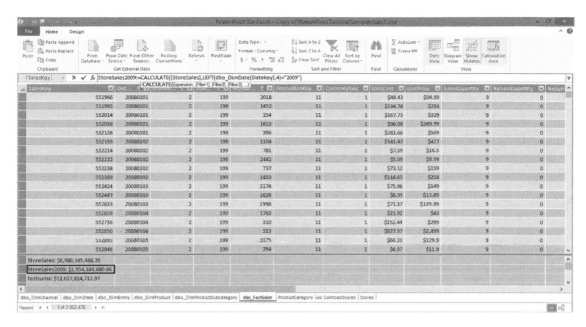

Figure 7-13. *Calculating the 2009 store sales*

3. Next, create a calculated field for store sales for the previous year, 2008, by entering the following DAX formula in the cell below, as shown in Figure 7-14.

```
StoreSales2008:=CALCULATE([StoreSales],LEFT(dbo_DimDate[Datekey],4)="2008")
```

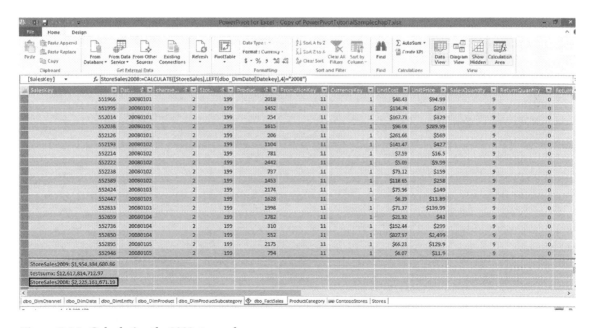

Figure 7-14. *Calculating the 2008 store sales*

4. Next, the year-over-year growth can be calculated by entering the following formula and changing the format to percent, as shown in Figure 7-15. The identifiers for the calculated fields have to be enclosed in square brackets. Note that sales decreased by 12% in 2009.

```
SalesChange:=([StoreSales2009]-[StoreSales2008])/[StoreSales2008]
```

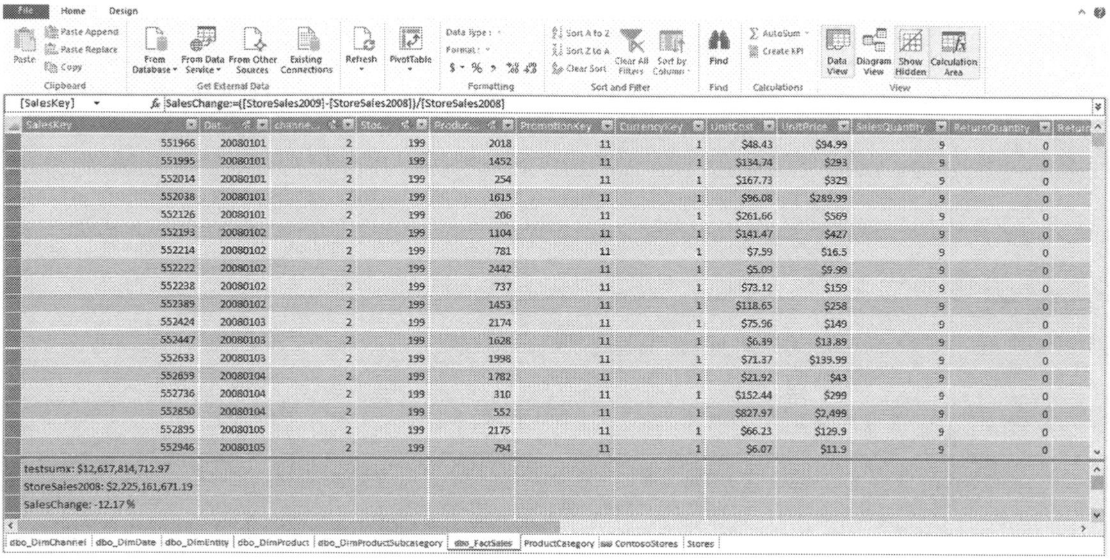

Figure 7-15. *Calculating a year or a year sales change*

Creating a KPI for Profitability

A KPI, or Key Performance Indicator, is based on the relationship between a calculated field and a value. Create a KPI for profitability by initiating the following steps:

1. Create a calculated field for average of profit/sales, as shown in Figure 7-16, by entering the following formula:

```
Average of Profit/Sales:=AVERAGE([Profit/Sales])
```

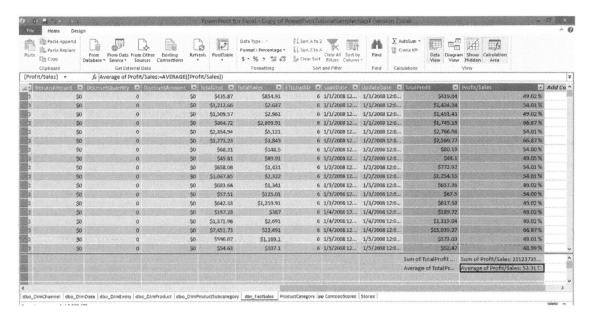

Figure 7-16. *Creating calculate field for Average of Profit/Sales*

2. Right-click the calculated field and select Create KPI. Enter an absolute value of
    .53, or 53%, and adjust the sliders so that green is displayed for values that meet
    the target, as shown in Figure 7-17, and click OK.

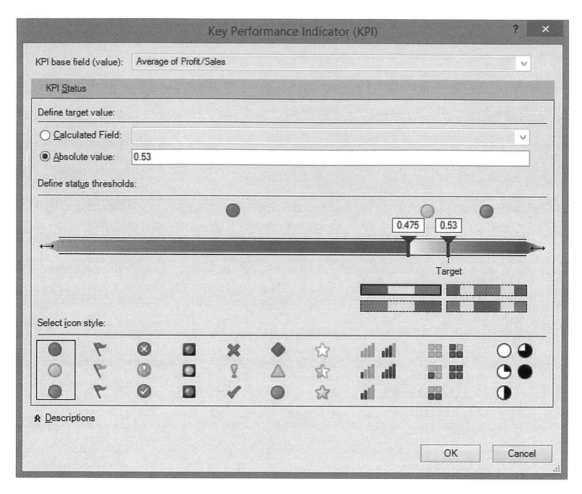

Figure 7-17. *Defining the KPI*

Creating a Pivot Table Showing Profitability by Product Line

To create a Pivot Table showing profitability by product line, follow these steps:

1. Select the dbo_FactSales tab.

2. Click the Pivot Table icon on the ribbon and select Pivot Table.

3. Select New Worksheet in the Create Pivot Table dialog and click OK.

4. Select the Product Category Name field in the Product Category table. It will appear in the Rows box in the Pivot Table pane on the right of the screen, as shown in Figure 7-18.

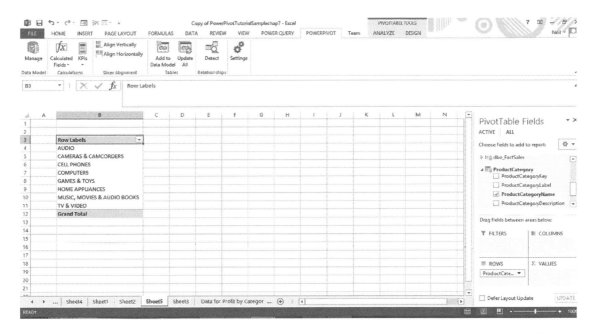

Figure 7-18. *Inserting product category name into Pivot Table*

5. Next, select the Sales Quantity field in the dbo_FactSales table and the Average of Profit/Sales calculated field, which appears at the bottom of the fields list. Click the calculated field name and select values, goal, and status. This field will appear in the values box, and a Pivot Table will be created, as shown in Figure 7-19.

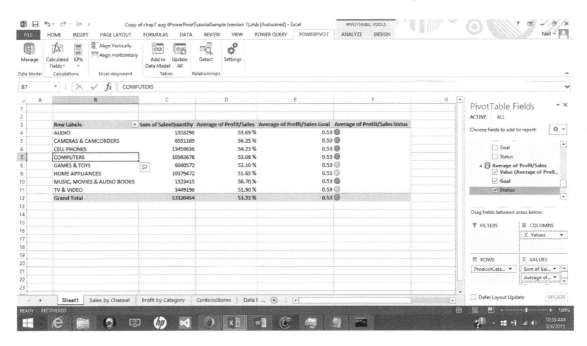

Figure 7-19. *Adding the KPI into Pivot Table*

Summary

This chapter showed how to use the DAX formula language to create calculated fields and calculated columns and how to create Key Performance Indicators to monitor business activity. In contrast to Excel formulas, which reference specific cells, DAX formulas reference columns, but the CALCULATE() function can be used to calculate an expression based on a filter.

■ ■ ■

Power Query

Microsoft Power Query for Excel is a data-discovery tool for importing data from a wide variety of sources, including relational, semi-structured, and unstructured data available from sources such as OData, Hadoop, and Azure Marketplace. It is a self-service ETL (export, transform, load) tool for extracting, transforming, and loading data. It is more powerful than some of the approaches that have been covered previously. Microsoft is constantly updating Power Query, so some features may have changed by the time this book is published. This chapter demonstrates how to access data—from the Web, in table format, CSV format, and JSON format—and then shape it using the Power Query editor before importing it into Excel.

Installing Power Query

If the Power Query tab is not visible, you will have to install it. Power Query is available as a free download from Microsoft for Excel 2010 and 2013. The download link can be accessed by doing a search on "Power Query download." Be sure to install the 32-bit version if you have installed the 32-bit version of Excel and the 64-bit version if you have the 64-bit version of Excel. To enable Power Query after installation, follow these steps:

1. Click the File tab to see the Backstage View.

2. Click Options at the bottom of the left pane.

3. Select Add-Ins on the left pane.

4. At the bottom of the window, pull down the arrow after Manage and select Com Add-Ins and click Go.

5. Check Microsoft Office PowerPivot for Excel 2013, Microsoft Power Map for Excel, and Power View, and click OK.

After installation, the Power Query tab will be visible.

Key Options on Power Query Ribbon

This section will cover the most useful options on the Power Query ribbon, which is shown in Figure 8-1.

Figure 8-1. *Power Query ribbon*

- *From Web*: Allows extracting tables from a specific web site

- *From File*: Imports from Excel, CSV, XML, text files, or from a group of files in a folder

- *From Database*: Imports from databases, such as SQL Server, Access, Oracle, and MySQL

- *From Azure*: Imports from Azure services, such as SQL Database, Market Place, HDInsight, Blob Storage, and Table Storage

- *From Other Sources*: Imports from sources including SharePoint Lists, OData feeds, Hadoop (HDFS), Facebook, Salesforce Objects and Reports, and ODBC

- *Recent Sources*: Shows the source of recent queries

- *From Table Excel Data*: Imports a range from an Excel spreadsheet

- *Merge*: Merges two queries to add columns

- *Append*: Appends one table to another with the same structure

- *Show Pane*: Toggles the display of the Workbook Query pane on the right side of the screen

- *Data Source Settings*: Manages setting for data sources that have been accessed through Power Query

- *Options*: Sets options for loading data

- *Update*: Checks online for Power Query updates

- *Data Catalog Search*: Searches a curated set of web sites and extracts tables

- *My Data Catalog Queries*: Allows sharing queries with other users

Working with the Query Editor

Power Query allows importing a subset of the data into the Query Editor, so that the data can be shaped by removing unneeded rows or columns or creating calculated columns before importing into Excel or into a data model. There are three tabs in Query Editor: Home, Transform, and Add Column.

Key Options on the Query Editor Home Ribbon

This section covers key options on the Query Editor Home ribbon, which is shown in Figure 8-2.

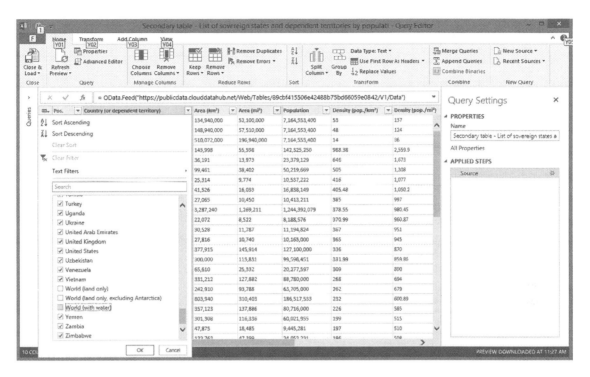

Figure 8-2. *Query Editor screen*

- *Close & Load*: Closes the editor and loads the data either into an Excel worksheet or into the data model

- *Refresh Preview*: Refreshes the query, reprocessing all steps, and previewing the results

- *Advanced Editor*: Shows the code used to extract the data in the M query language

- *Choose Columns/Remove Columns*: Allows keeping or removing selected columns. Clicking the Choose Columns icon will show a list of columns that can be unchecked to remove, as shown in Figure 8-3.

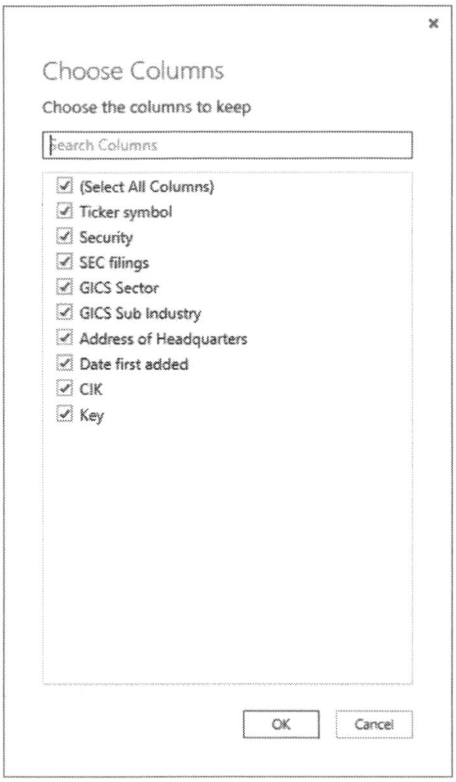

Figure 8-3. *Choose Columns dialog*

- *Keep Rows/Remove Rows*: Allows keeping or removing selected rows

- *Remove Duplicates*: Removes duplicates. Be careful about defining the criteria for duplicates. For example, in a list of stock prices by day, removing duplicates based only on the stock symbol would leave only one unique row for each stock.

- *Sort*: Sorts columns in ascending or descending order. Remember that the Query Editor is only working a subset of the data. It might be better to wait until the data is loaded into a worksheet or data model before sorting.

- *Split Column*: Splits columns based on a delimiter, such as a comma or space

- *Group By*: Groups rows based on a field or fields

Note that another way to remove or filter out rows is by clicking the arrow to the right of the column heading and de-selecting values, as shown in Figure 8-2.

A Simple Population

This example will show how to use the Data Catalog Search option to retrieve population data in a tabular format for analysis. The Data Catalog Search option searches a curated data catalog of public data web sites, such as Wikipedia and the Census Bureau web site, and allows tables to be easily extracted from those web sites. It is not a full-featured search engine. It seems to understand searches that start with words such as *largest* or *most*. It can also search corporate databases after being logged in to the corporate network. For this example, take the following steps.

1. On the Power Query tab, click Data Catalog Search.

2. In the Search pane to the right, enter "most populated countries." Hover the mouse pointer over the results to get a preview of the data. Then hover the mouse over the item in the list entitled "Secondary table—List of sovereign states and dependent territories by population density" from Wikipedia. The results are shown in Figure 8-4. Note the prompts at the bottom for Load and Edit.

Figure 8-4. *Preview of population data*

3. Click Edit on the lower left of the preview to load a subset of data from the table into the Query Editor, as shown in Figure 8-5. The table lists countries with their population and areas in square miles or square kilometers and shows their population density per square mile or square kilometer.

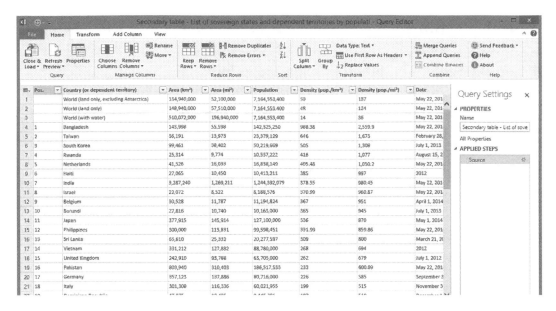

Figure 8-5. Population data in Query Editor

4. In the Query Editor, data can be manipulated by deleting rows or columns, splitting or merging columns, or removing duplicates. For example, to delete the columns for area or density in kilometers, select both columns by clicking the header of the first column to be deleted and Ctrl-click the header of the second column, as shown in Figure 8-6.

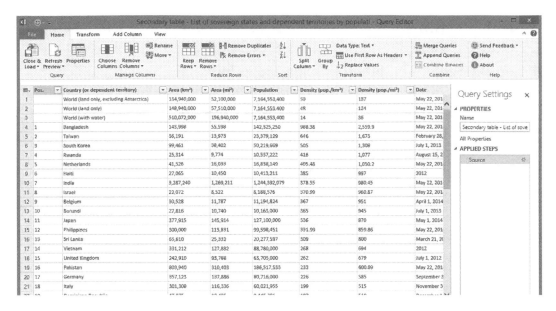

Figure 8-6. Highlighting columns for deletion

5. Then click Remove Columns under Remove Columns on the tab, to remove the selected columns.

6. After the data is shaped the way you want, click Close & Load, to load the data into an Excel spreadsheet.

Performance of S&P 500 Stock Index

This example will show how to retrieve S&P 500 performance data, by taking the following steps:

1. On the Power Query ribbon, click Data Catalog Search.

2. In the search box, type "S&P 500 performance." Hover the mouse over the first link, labeled "Total annual returns...," as shown in Figure 8-7.

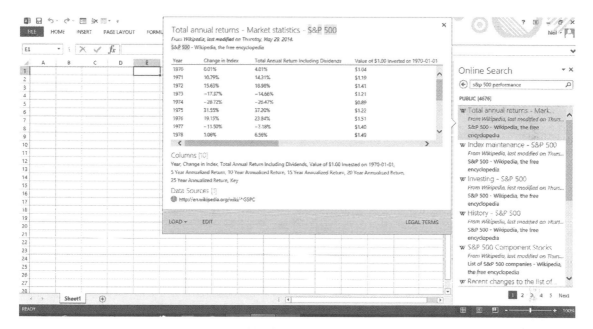

Figure 8-7. *Data preview*

3. Click Edit in the lower left to load the data showing S&P 500 returns for every year from 1970 to 2013 into the Query Editor, as shown in Figure 8-8.

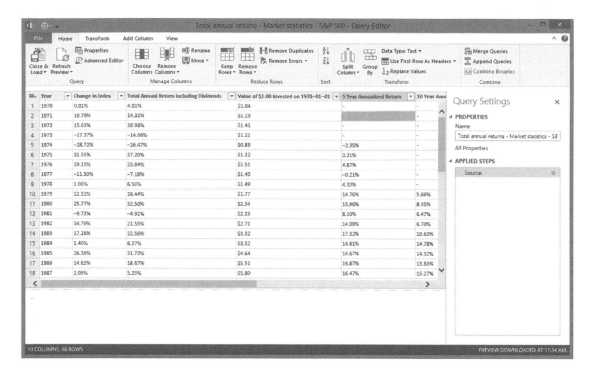

Figure 8-8. *Data in Query Editor*

4. Select the columns by clicking Choose Columns and unchecking columns that will not be included. For this example, the 5-, 10-, 15-, and 20-year return columns will be removed, as shown in Figure 8-9. Click OK.

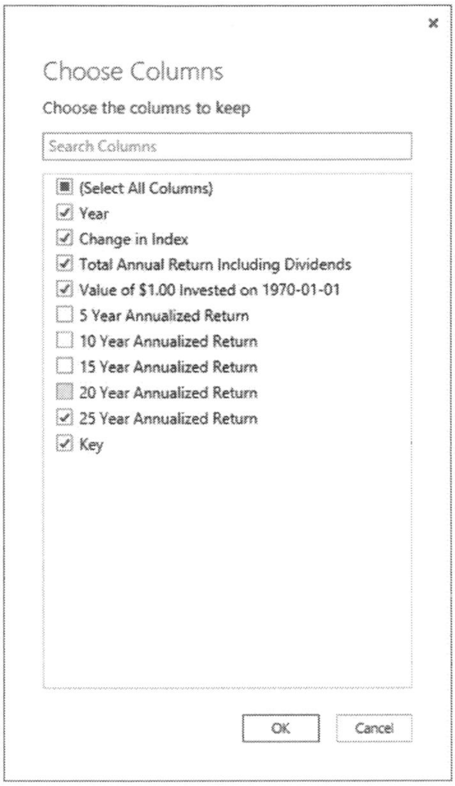

Figure 8-9. *Choose Columns dialog*

5. To remove the four bottom rows, click Remove Rows and then Remove Bottom Rows and enter 4 as the number of rows to be removed, as shown in Figure 8-10, and click OK.

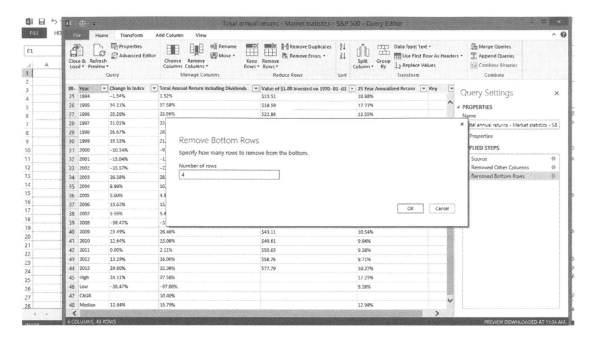

Figure 8-10. *Remove Rows dialog*

6. Then click Close & Load on the left side of the ribbon to import the data into a
spreadsheet, to get the results shown in Figure 8-11.

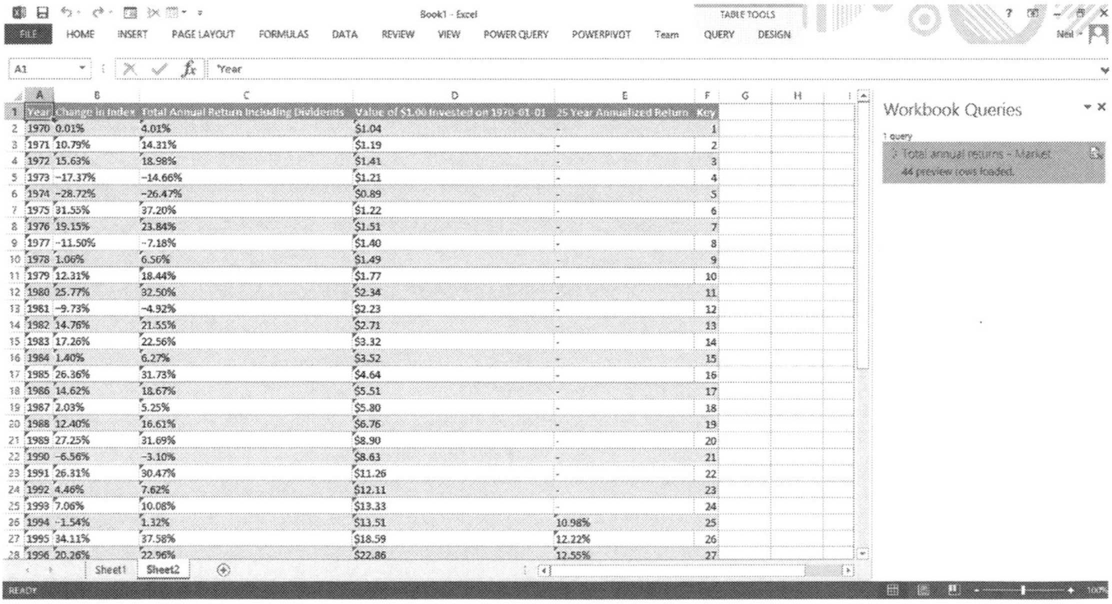

Figure 8-11. *Data imported into a spreadsheet*

Importing CSV Files from a Folder

Sometimes Hadoop data will be stored in files with comma-separated values. Rather than loading it into Hortonworks Sandbox or some other product to be manipulated as a Hadoop, the files with comma-separated values can be loaded directly into Excel and PowerPivot, using Power Query. The following example demonstrates how to do this.

1. First download the stock market zipped file from the following URL:

    s3.amazonaws.com/hortonassets/mstut/nyse.zip

2. After the download is complete, double-click the file in your browsers download window to open it, as shown in Figure 8-12.

Figure 8-12. *Download window*

3. Two folders of .csv files will be downloaded, as shown in Figure 8-13.

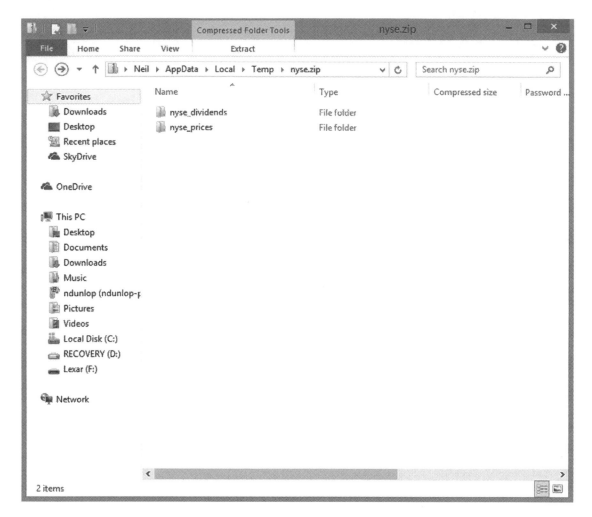

Figure 8-13. Windows showing file folders

4. Drag the folder nyse_prices to the desktop, to make it easier to access.

5. Open Excel and click the Power Query tab. Select From File and From Folder, as shown in Figure 8-14.

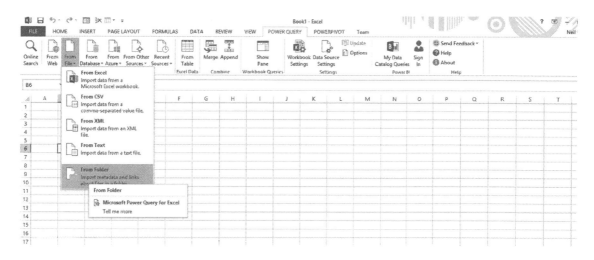

Figure 8-14. *Power Query screen to import from File Folder*

6. Click Browse and select the nyse_prices folder from the desktop, as shown in Figure 8-15. Click OK.

Figure 8-15. *Folder screen*

The result is a list of .csv files, as shown in Figure 8-16.

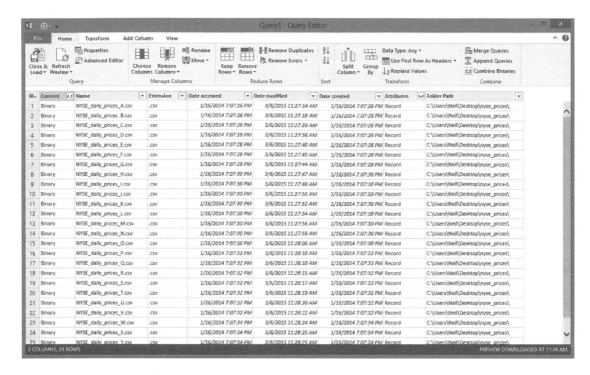

Figure 8-16. *List of* .csv *files*

7. To open a file, click Binary in the leftmost column. For this example, select the file in the fifth row. The file is opened in the QueryEditor, and results are shown in Figure 8-17. Remember that the Query Editor can only contain a subset of the total number of records.

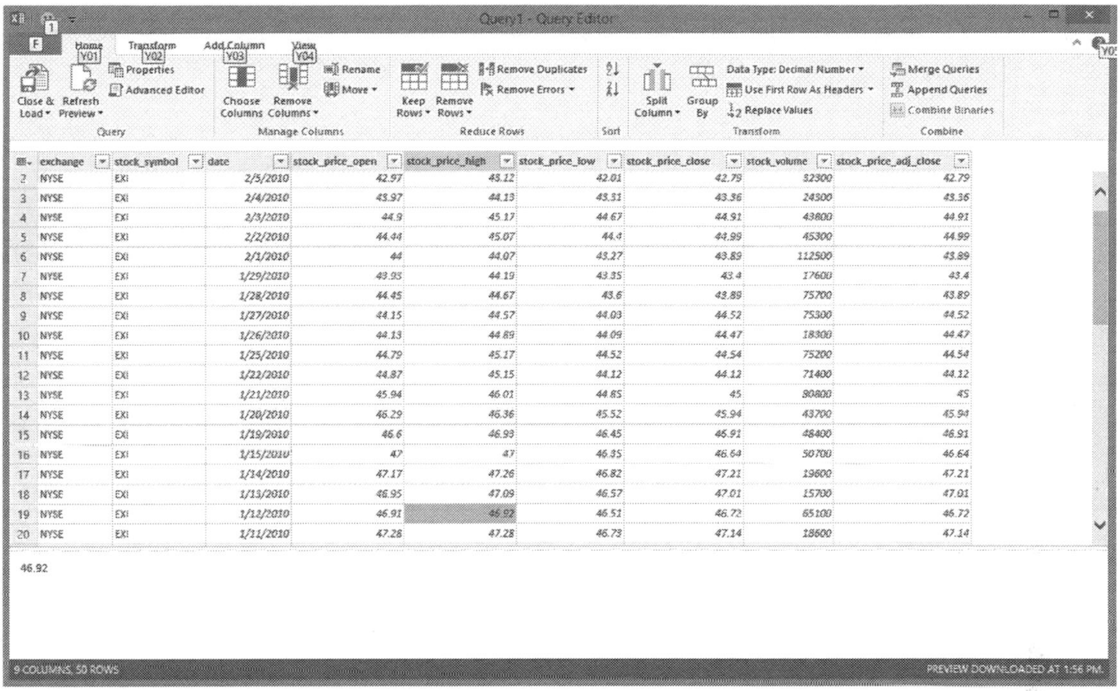

Figure 8-17. *CSV file imported into Query Editor*

8. Note that this file contains the opening, high, low, and closing stock price and volume for each stock on a given day. For this example, all rows and columns will be retained.

9. Click Close & Load to load the records from the Query Editor into a spreadsheet. The results are shown in Figure 8-18.

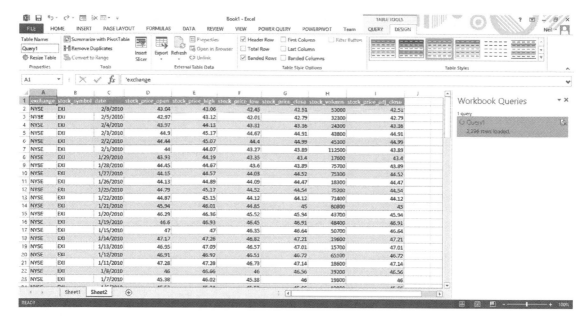

Figure 8-18. *Data loaded into spreadsheet*

Group By

To group by a specific category, go into the Query Editor and follow these steps:

1. Reopen the Query Editor, by clicking Launch Editor on the Power Query tab. Then click Transform and Select Group By at the left end of the ribbon.

2. In the Group By dialog, select the stock_symbol column as the Group By criteria and leave the default as Count, as shown in Figure 8-19.

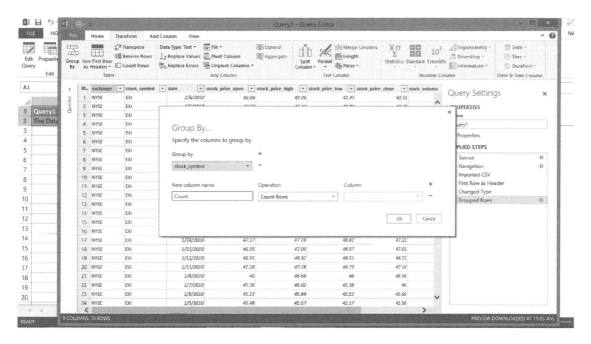

Figure 8-19. *Group By dialog*

3. Click OK, and the results shown in Figure 8-20 will appear.

Figure 8-20. *Results after doing a Group By on stock_symbol*

Importing JSON

This example shows how to use Power Query to extract JSON data from a web site. Figure 8-21 shows the raw JSON data on Nobel Prize winners.

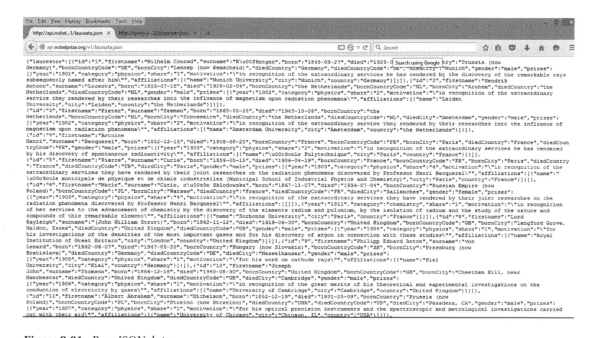

Figure 8-21. *Raw JSON data*

To import the data using Power Query, follow these steps:

1. Click the Power Query tab.

2. Click From Web and enter the following URL, as shown in Figure 8-22, and click OK:

```
http://api.nobelprize.org/v1/laureate.json
```

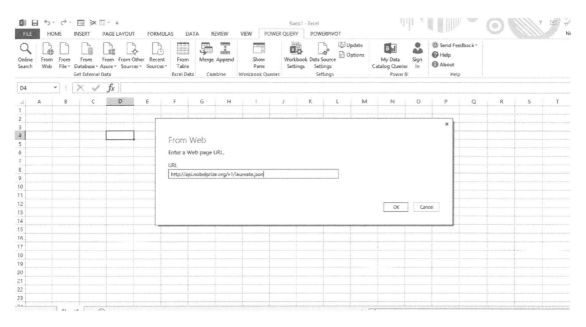

Figure 8-22. *Importing using the From Web option*

> 3. The Query Editor will open. Click the Into Table icon at the upper left of the ribbon, as shown in Figure 8-23.

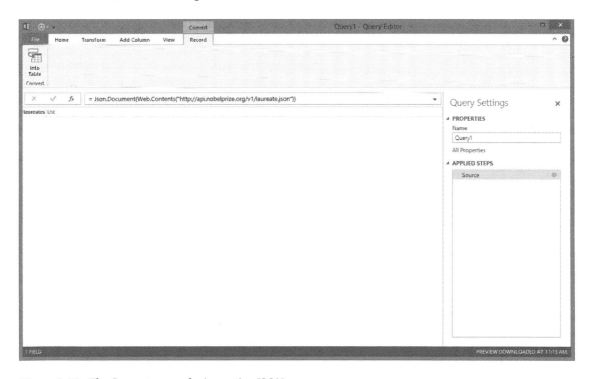

Figure 8-23. *The Convert screen for importing JSON*

4. The result, which displays only the column heading, is shown in Figure 8-24.

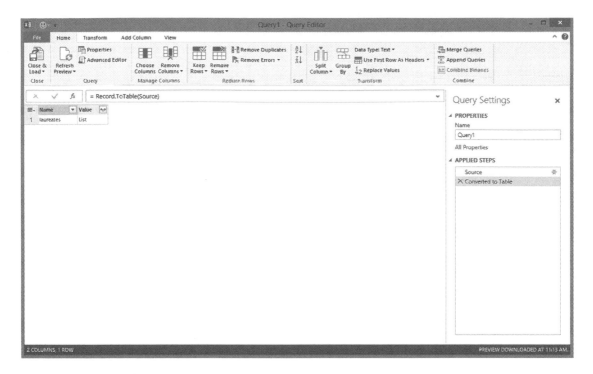

Figure 8-24. *Top-level JSON import*

5. Notice the expand button to the right of Value. Click that expand button. The results are shown in Figure 8-25.

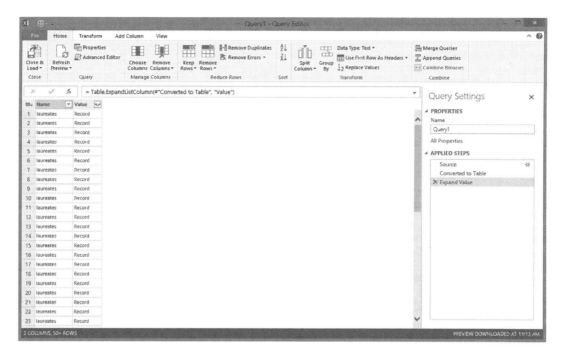

Figure 8-25. *JSON column list*

6. Click the expand button again. The results are shown in Figure 8-26.

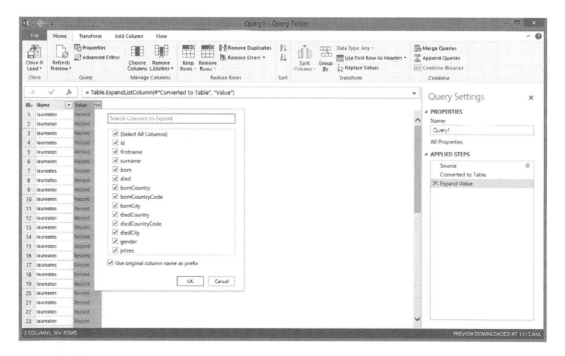

Figure 8-26. *Select columns dialog box*

7. Accept the defaults and click OK to get the results shown in Figure 8-27, which shows the actual records, with a single row for each Nobel laureate.

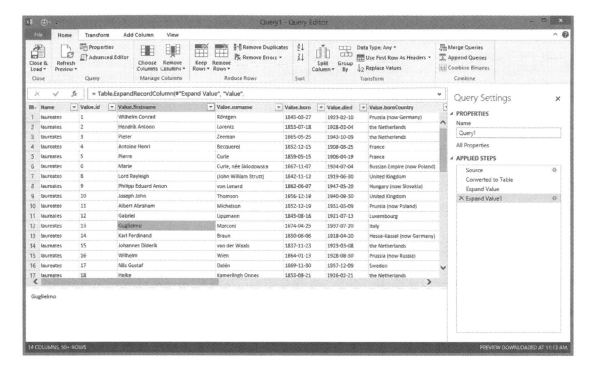

Figure 8-27. JSON data in rows and columns.

8. Scroll all the way to the right to find another expand button, as shown in Figure 8-28.

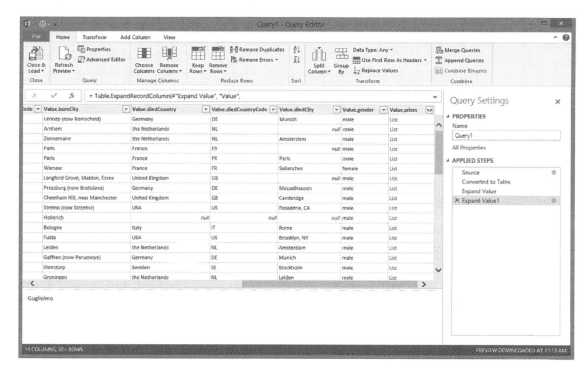

Figure 8-28. *Additonal columns*

9. Clicking this expand button will generate multiple rows for persons who won the Nobel Prize more than once, as shown in Figure 8-29.

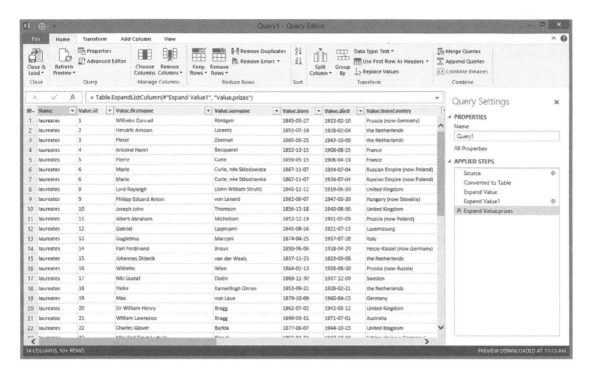

Figure 8-29. *Expanded view with multiple rows for recipients of multiple Nobel Prizes*

10. Scrolling to the right, clicking the expand button again, and accepting the defaults, as shown in Figure 8-30, will expand some of the fields that were not shown before, such as the reason for the prize.

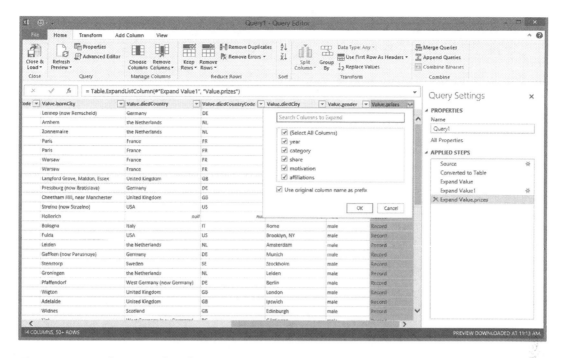

Figure 8-30. *Further expanding the rows*

11. The results are shown in Figure 8-31.

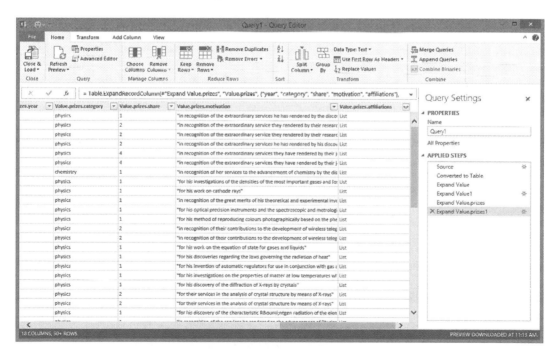

Figure 8-31. *Display showing reason (motivation) for Nobel Prize*

12. Decisions can be made about how to group the data. For example, to group the data by category, click the heading of the category column to select the desired category, then right-click and select Group By to see the Group By... dialog, as shown in Figure 8-32.

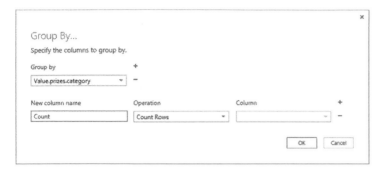

Figure 8-32. *Group By... dialog with single field*

13. Clicking OK will show a count of the prizes by category, as in Figure 8-33.

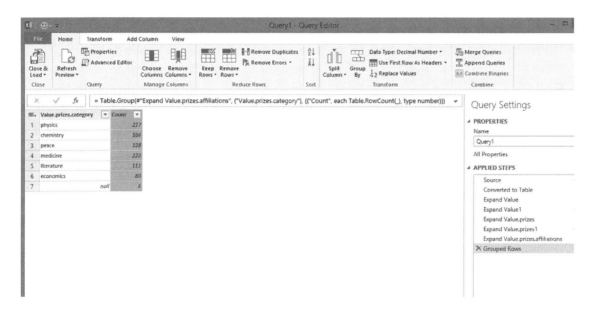

Figure 8-33. *Count of Nobel Prizes by category*

14. It is possible to group by two fields, such as category and year, by clicking the plus sign in the Group By... dialog box to select a second field, as shown in Figure 8-34. The Group By... dialog box can be accessed again by clicking the gear icon after Group Rows at the bottom of the Applied Steps list in the Query Setting pane on the right side of the screen.

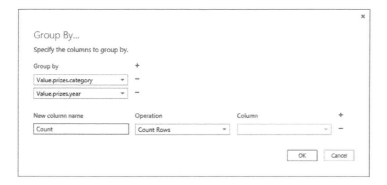

Figure 8-34. *Group By dialog with two fields*

15. The results are shown in Figure 8-35.

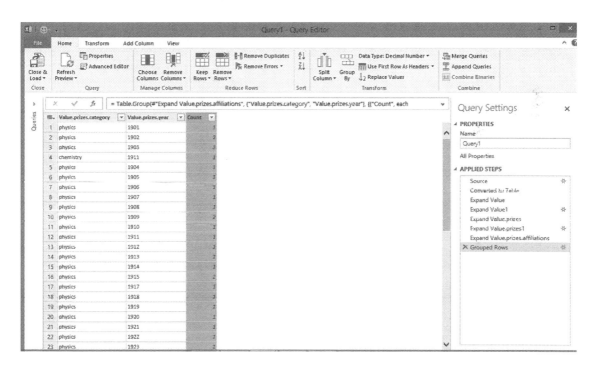

Figure 8-35. *Count of Nobel Prizes by category and year*

16. To add a third field to show the name of the prize winner, select + again in the Group By... dialog and add the surname of the winner, as shown in Figure 8-36.

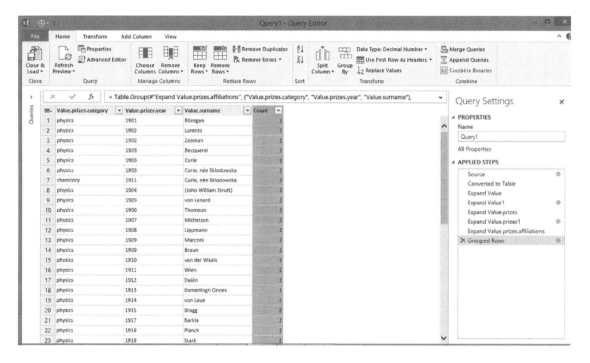

Figure 8-36. *Group By... dialog with three fields*

17. The results are shown in Figure 8-37.

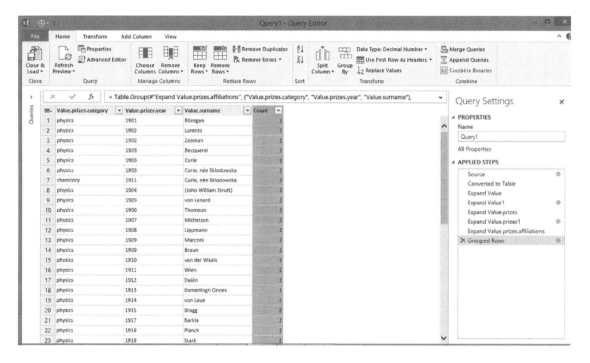

Figure 8-37. *Display of Nobel Prizes by category and year, with surname of recipient*

Summary

This chapter has demonstrated how to use Power Query to import tables from web sites, multiple CSV files from a folder, and JSON data. The examples have shown how to use Power Query to extract, transform, and load data. More examples of using Power Query will be provided in later chapters.

CHAPTER 9

■ ■ ■

Power Map

Power Map is a powerful visualization tool that allows the creation of 2D and 3D visualizations by plotting Excel-based geospatial data on a map, using Bing Map technology. This chapter demonstrates how to import data using Power Query and then how to plot it using Power Map.

Installing Power Map

Power Map is accessed through an icon on the Excel Insert tab. If that icon is not displayed, it may mean that you do not have the version of Power Map installed. If that is the case, do a search on "download Power Map" and download the latest version from Microsoft. Then, to enable Power Map, follow these steps:

1. Click the File tab to see the Backstage View.

2. Click Options at the bottom of the left pane.

3. Select Add-Ins on the left pane.

4. At the bottom of the window, pull down the arrow after Manage, select Com Add-Ins, and click Go.

5. Check Microsoft Office PowerPivot for Excel 2013, Microsoft Power Map for Excel and Power View, and click OK.

Plotting a Map

The steps to plotting a map include the following:

1. Open a data source, which may be a spreadsheet or a data model that includes geographic descriptors, such as city and state or geographic coordinates.

2. Select the Insert tab and click Map and Load Power Map.

3. In the Fields list pane on the right side of the screen, select geographic fields to map to, such as city and state or geographic coordinates, and then select a data metric, such as population. Power Map calls Bing Map services to locate the geographic locations on a map, and then the metric value is plotted.

4. By default, a column chart is displayed. This can be changed to a bubble chart or heat map by clicking the appropriate icon.

A Power Map video tour is an animation that tells a story about data by linking individual maps. A video can be created to tell a story based on the data. A video is a collection of tours, and a tour is a collection of scenes.

Key Power Map Ribbon Options

This section highlights some of the key options on the Power Map ribbon, which is shown in Figure 9-1.

Figure 9-1. *Power Map ribbon*

- Tour Section
  - Play Tour. Plays a tour already created
  - Add Scene. Adds a scene to a tour
  - Create Video. Creates a video from tours
- Map Section
  - Themes. Changes the map style
  - Map Labels. Adds country or city names
  - Flat Map. Switches between 2D and 3D views
- Layer Section
  - Add Layer. Adds a new layer
  - Refresh Data. Refreshes data from the source
  - Shapes. Selects the shape of the bar chart
- Insert Section
  - 2D Chart. Adds a 2D chart
  - Text Box. Adds a text box on the map
  - Legend. Adds a legend to the map
- Time Section
  - Time Line. Shows or hides the time line in a time animation
  - Date & Time. Shows or adds the date and time in a time animation
- View Section
  - Tour Editor. Displays or hides the Tour Editor pane (left side of screen)
  - Layer Pane. Displays or hides the Layer Pane (right side of screen)

Troubleshooting

Power Map is very particular about data types. If numeric data that you want to plot is not treated as numeric data, as evidenced by only showing a count aggregation, or if time data is not recognized, follow these steps:

1. Check for any extraneous string data in the column and delete the row containing string data.

2. Make sure that a numeric data column is formatted as a number and that a date column is formatted as date.

3. After changing the format, click Refresh Data on the Power Map ribbon.

EXERCISE 9-1. MAPPING CALIFORNIA CRIME STATISTICS EXAMPLE

This example shows how to use Power Query to import California crime statistics by city and how to use Power Map to plot the data.

1. Go to Power Query and do a Data Catalog search on "California Cities by Population and Crime Rate." Hover your mouse over "Cities—California locations by crime rate" and select Edit to load into the Query Editor. The screen shown in Figure 9-2 will appear.

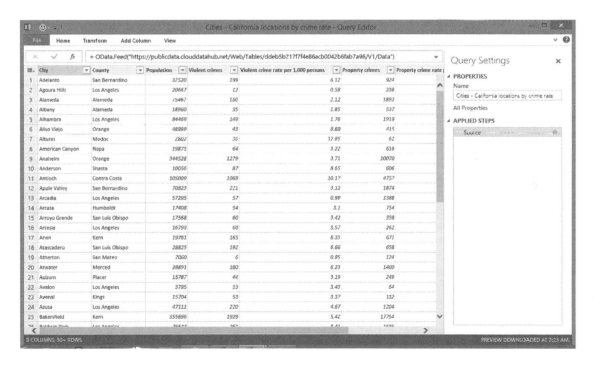

Figure 9-2. *Crime Statistics in Query Editor*

2. In Query Editor, click the Add Column tab. On the left end of the tab, click Add Custom Column. Create a new column for state. Set the contents `="CA"`, as shown in Figure 9-3.

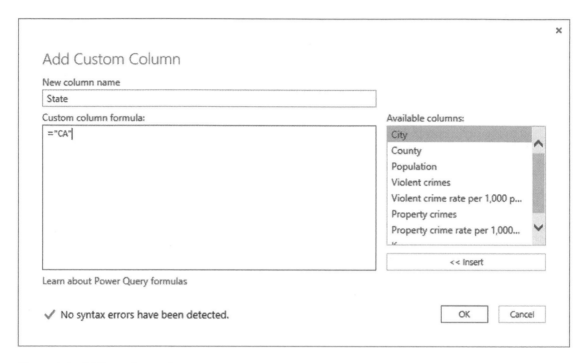

Figure 9-3. *Adding a State column*

3. Check that the data type of all the numeric columns is a decimal number by right-clicking the column heading, selecting Change Type, and selecting Decimal Number. Also, check that there are no non-numeric values in numeric columns. When the data is the way you want it, click Close & Load on the ribbon, to load to a spreadsheet. The spreadsheet should appear as shown in Figure 9-4.

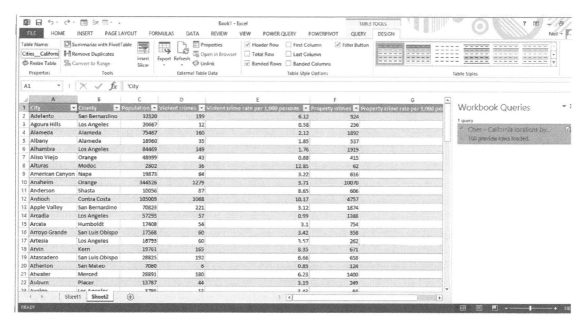

Figure 9-4. *Crime data loaded into spreadsheet*

Again, check for non-numeric values in number fields that could keep Power Map from interpreting the contents correctly. Because not all the rows are displayed in the Query Editor, for larger datasets, this has to be checked after loading the data into Excel. As shown in Figure 9-5, the last row of data may contain ellipses. If this is the case, delete that last row by right-clicking the row and selecting Delete Table Row.

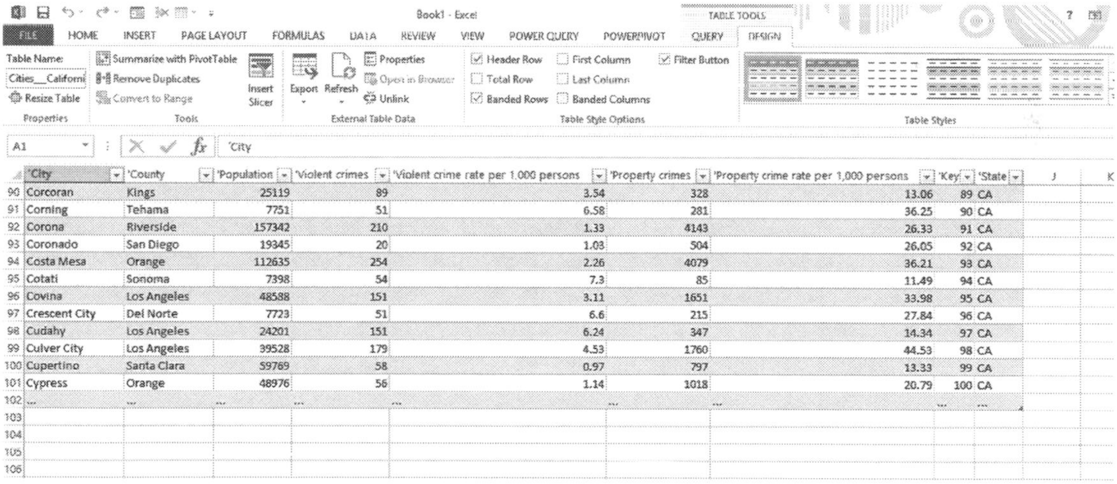

Figure 9-5. *Ellipsis in the last row that has to be deleted*

4. Check the formatting of each column by highlighting the column, by clicking the letter at the top of the column. Right-click the selected column and select Format Cells from the Context menu. For the population, violent crimes, and property crimes columns, set the format to Number, with 0 places to the right of the point, as shown in Figure 9-6. For the violent crimes and property crimes per 1,000 persons, set the format to Number, with 2 places to the right of the point.

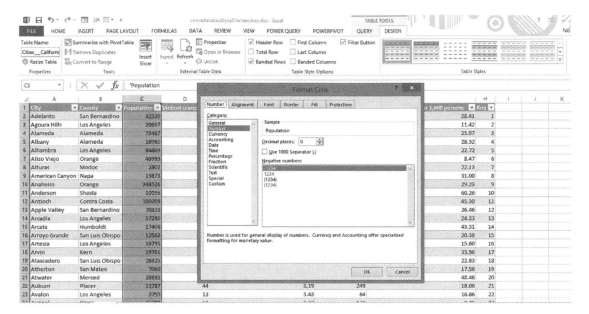

Figure 9-6. *Formatting column as number*

5. Click the Insert tab and select Launch Power Map under Map. If you have previously created a map, you may be prompted to create a New Tour. Accept the default of City, County, and State as the geographic fields, as shown in Figure 9-7. Click Next.

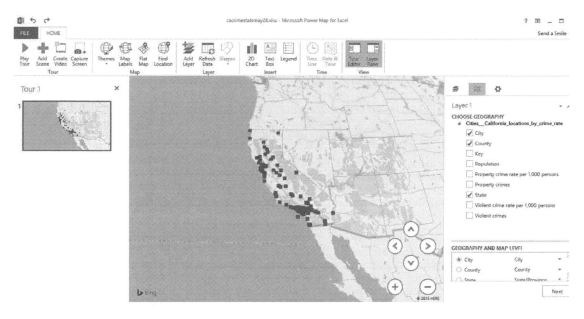

Figure 9-7. *Setting the geogrpahic fields*

6. Click Map Labels on the ribbon to display city names. In the Layer pane, right-click
    Property Crimes per 1,000 persons and then click Add to Height, as shown in
    Figure 9-8. Note that the Bing Mapping service is showing a certainty of 94% for
    the geographic mapping in the upper right corner. If you want to go back and edit
    the geographic fields, click the icon above the 94%.

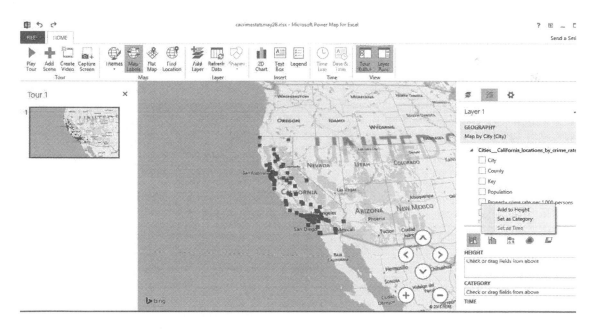

Figure 9-8. *Setting field for height of plot*

7. Click the legend box and resize it to be smaller, then drag it to the upper left part of the map. Click the large + on the lower right side of the map several times to zoom in. The results are shown in Figure 9-9. Note that it is possible to point the mouse at any graphic, to see the details about that city crime rate. It is also possible to double-click any location, to zoom in.

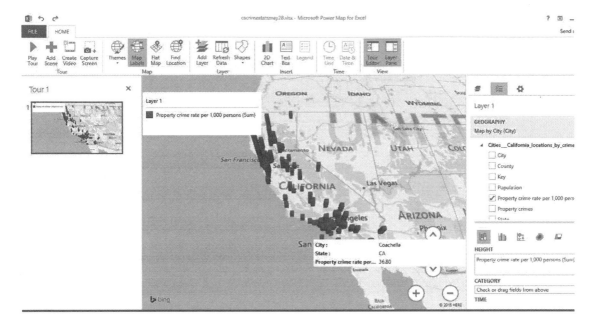

Figure 9-9. *Map with legend and detailed crime statistics*

Plotting Multiple Statistics

It is possible to plot multiple metrics—both property crime and violent crime statistics. To do this, let's continue with the example from the preceding section.

EXERCISE 9-2. MAPPING CALIFORNIA CRIME STATISTICS, PART 2

You can plot the property crime and violent crime statistics by following these steps:

1. In the Layer pane, right-click Property crime rate per 1,000 persons and select Add to Height, as shown in Figure 9-10.

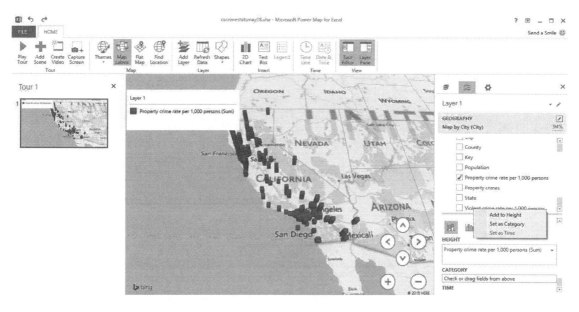

Figure 9-10. *Adding violent crimes metric*

2. Note that the default view is stacked column. This can be changed to clustered column by clicking the icon to the right of stacked column, as shown in Figure 9-11. The property crime rate is shown in blue, and the violent crime rate in orange.

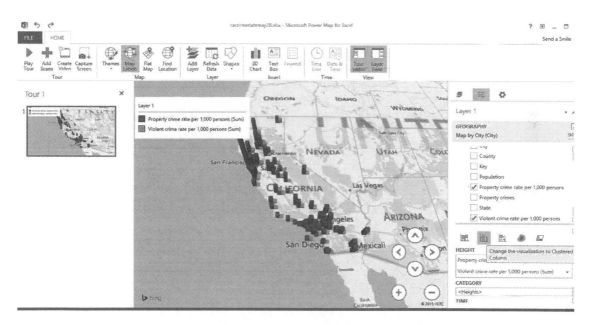

Figure 9-11. *Display of both property crime and violent crime metric*

3. Click Add Scene on the left end of the ribbon.

4. Click the Text Box icon on the ribbon and add the title "California Cities Crime Rates," as shown in Figure 9-12.

Figure 9-12. *Adding a title to the map*

5. Change the view to the bubble view, which is like a pie chart. The text box can be resized and dragged to the appropriate location on the map, as shown in Figure 9-13.

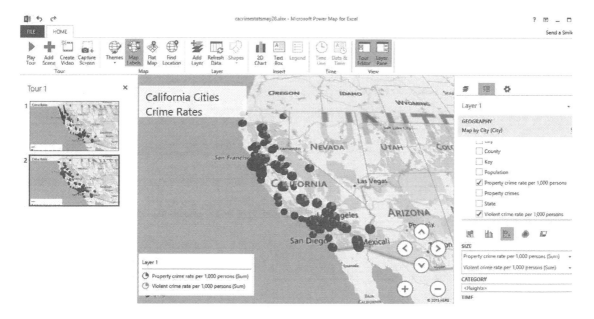

Figure 9-13. *Bubble view of data*

6.   The size of the bubbles can be adjusted by clicking the gear icon at the top right of the Layer pane, selecting Layer Options, and adjusting the size slider, as shown in Figure 9-14.

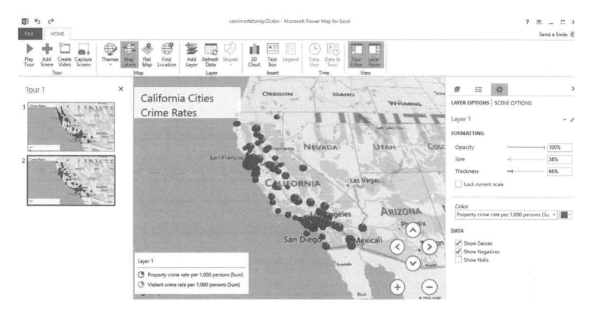

Figure 9-14. *Adusting bubble size*

7.   Click the Add Scene on the left end of the ribbon.

8.   Another view is the heat map view shown in Figure 9-15. Note that San Francisco and Los Angeles, the two largest cities in California, have the most crime.

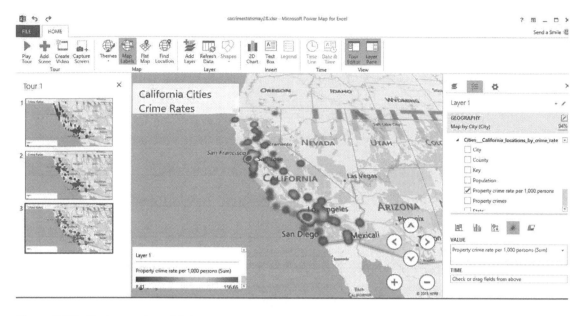

Figure 9-15. *Heat map view of data*

Adding a 2D Chart

A two dimensional chart for Property crime rate per 1,000 persons can be added by clicking 2D Chart on the ribbon. The results are shown in Figure 9-16.

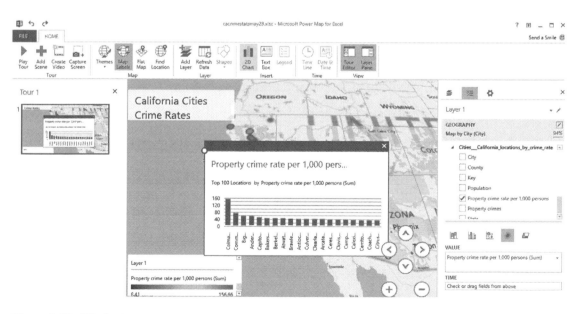

Figure 9-16. *2D chart*

EXERCISE 9-3. PLOTTING EUROPEAN UNEMPLOYMENT RATES EXAMPLE

This example will show how to load data about European unemployment rates into Power Query and how to plot it using Power Map. It will also show how to unpivot data in order to add a time animation. Follow these steps:

1. Click the Power Query tab and select Data Catalog Search.

2. Type "European Unemployment" into the search box. Hover the mouse over each of the results to get a preview of the data, as shown in Figure 9-17.

Figure 9-17. *Preview of European unemployment data*

3. Select Edit, at the bottom of the preview screen, to load the data into the Query Editor, as shown in Figure 9-18.

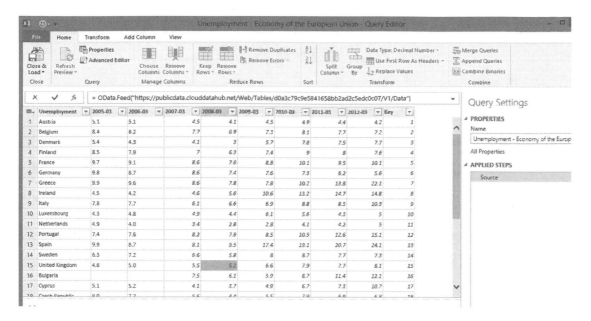

Figure 9-18. Unemployment data in Query Editor

4. Check the shape of the data to see if there any extraneous columns. In this case, the columns include the country names and the unemployment rate by year and a key column that uses sequential numbering. Also, check the rows. Notice that there are rows for US and Japanese unemployment, as well as European.

5. Also, check the data type for each column to see if it is the correct type. To check the data type, select the column by clicking the heading and note the data type shown in the upper right section of the ribbon. To change the data type, select a column, click the arrow after Data Type on the ribbon, and select the correct data type. Notice that the data type for 2005 and 2006 is text and that for the other years is Decimal Number. Use this approach to change the type of all numeric columns to Decimal Number.

6. Check the column headings. Notice that the heading for the column with the country names is Unemployment, which is not descriptive. To change the column name, right-click the column heading and select Rename. Rename it to country, as shown in Figure 9-19. Notice that the column rename is listed under Applied Steps in the Query Settings pane on the right side of the screen.

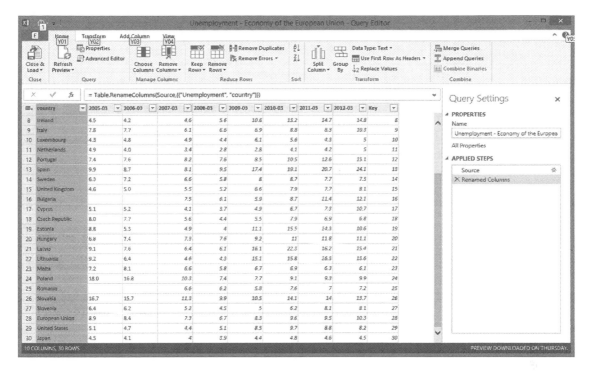

Figure 9-19. *Query Editor after renaming country column*

7. When the data is shaped the way you want it, select Close & Load at the leftmost side of the Query Editor ribbon to load the data into a spreadsheet. Note that data can also be loaded into a Data Model, but for this example, a spreadsheet will be used.

8. This would be a good time to save the spreadsheet and name it "European Unemployment."

9. To start the mapping, select the Insert tab and Map and then Launch Power Map.

10. The screen shown in Figure 9-20 will appear. Note that in the Layer pane, on the right side of the screen, country is selected as the geographic field. Click Next.

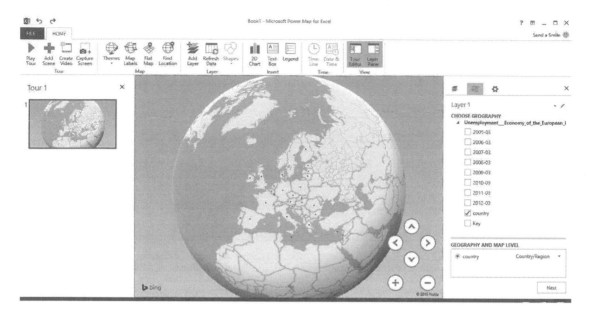

Figure 9-20. *Country selected as geographic field*

11. Note that dots appear in each country that has data. Click Map Labels on the ribbon
to display country names and select the numeric field that will be plotted. In this
case, the 2012 unemployment rate will be checked, so that it can be plotted, as
shown in Figure 9-21. Note that when the field is checked, it is added to the Height
box. The default format is stacked column, and the default aggregation of the
numeric values is sum. Pointing the mouse at a column on the map will display the
unemployment rate for that country in 2012.

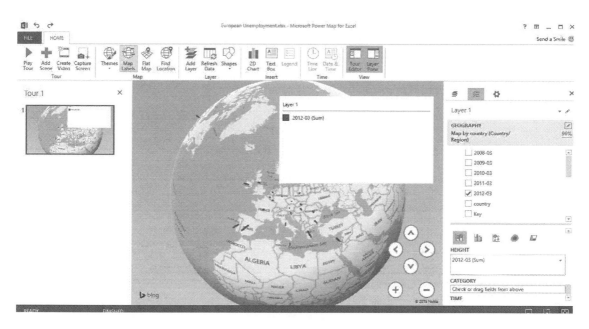

Figure 9-21. *2012 unemployment shown as a bar chart*

12. Change the aggregation to none by clicking the arrow at the right side of the Height box and selecting No Aggregation. Resize the legend box by clicking it and using the handles, and drag it to reposition it on the left side of the map, as shown in Figure 9-22.

Figure 9-22. *Map after moving legend box and changing aggregation to none*

13. Experiment with the different visualization formats by clicking the icons above the word *Height* in the Layer pane, to view the clustered column, bubble, heat map, and region. Note that because only one set of data is being shown, the clustered column and stacked column format are the same. A bubble view is shown in Figure 9-23.

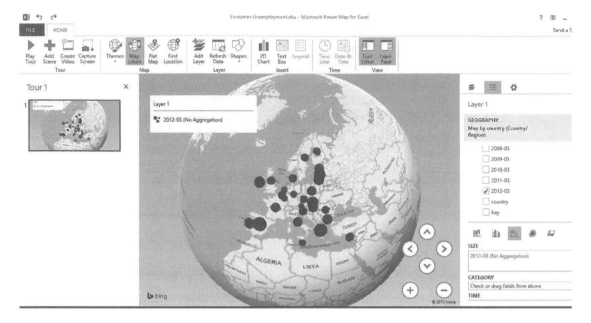

Figure 9-23. *Bubble view*

14. To zoom in on a map, click the large + sign at the bottom right of the map or double-click an area of the map to zoom in.

15. To change the opacity, size, or thickness of the bubble, click the gear icon on the right, at the top of the Layer pane. Figure 9-24 shows a heat map view with the color scale set to 180%, the radius of the heat map to 191%, and opacity at 99%. The legend box for Layer 1 shows the color key based on the unemployment rate. Note that you can also decide whether to show zeroes, negatives, and nulls, by checking or unchecking the box.

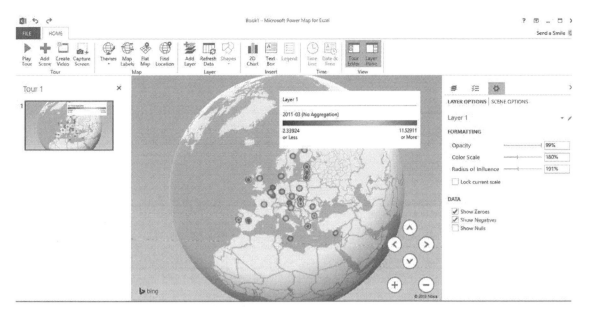

Figure 9-24. *Heat map view*

Showing Two or More Values

Two or more values can be displayed, such as showing unemployment rates in two different years. Using the example from the preceding section, Figure 9-25 shows the employment rates for 2011 (orange) and 2012 (blue) as a bubble. Pointing the mouse at the color on the bubble will show the unemployment rate for that year.

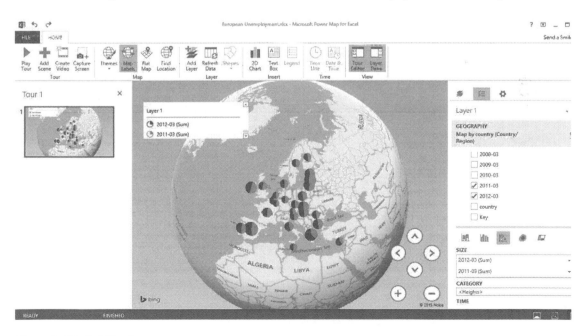

Figure 9-25. *Bubble view*

Figure 9-26 shows the unemployment rates for 2010 (orange) and 2011 (blue) as stacked bar columns. Pointing the mouse at the color on the stacked bar will show the unemployment rate for that year.

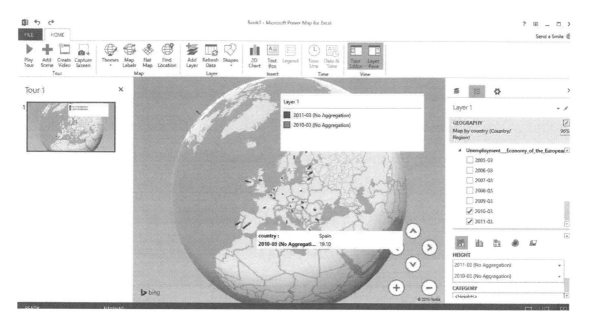

Figure 9-26. *Stacked bar view*

The same data shown with clustered columns, where the columns are side-by-side, is shown in Figure 9-27.

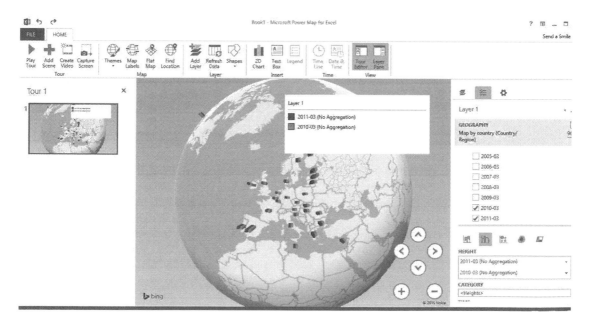

Figure 9-27. *Clustered column view*

Creating a 2D Chart

A two-dimensional chart showing the progression over time can be plotted by checking a series of years and then clicking 2D Chart on the ribbon. The result is shown in Figure 9-28. Hovering the mouse over the 2D chart will bring up a box with a down arrow after the title, which allows changing the chart type.

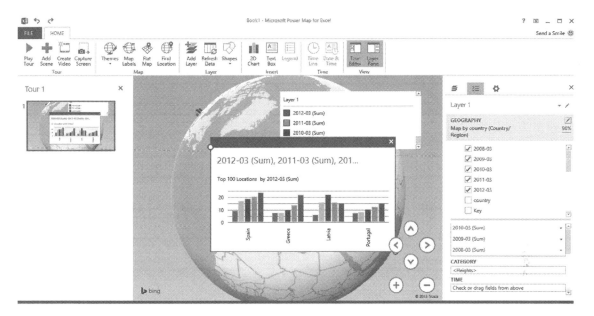

Figure 9-28. *2D chart*

EXERCISE 9-4. BUILDING A TIME ANIMATION EXERCISE

It is possible to animate a presentation to show the map values at different times. To do this, it is necessary to unpivot the data to indicate that a value is shown for each country for each year. To start from scratch, go back to steps 1–3 at the beginning of "Exercise 9-3. Plotting European Unemployment Rates Example" to load the data into the Query Editor, or click Recent Sources on the PowerPivot tab and select the data there.

1.   In the Query Editor, click the first year column heading to select the column. Then Ctrl-click the other year column headings to select all year columns, or after selecting the first year column, Shift-click the last year column to select all year columns. Right-click one of the selected column headings and select Unpivot Columns, as shown in Figure 9-29.

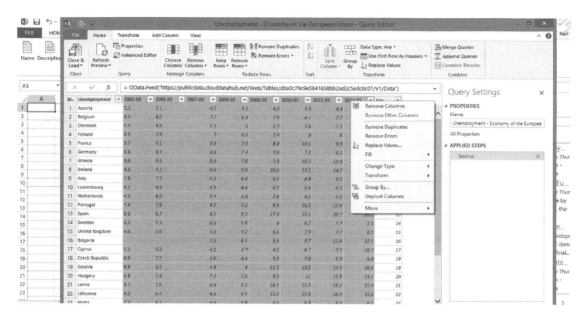

Figure 9-29. *Context menu showing the Unpivot Columns option*

2. The results are shown in Figure 9-30. One row has been created for each country and year.

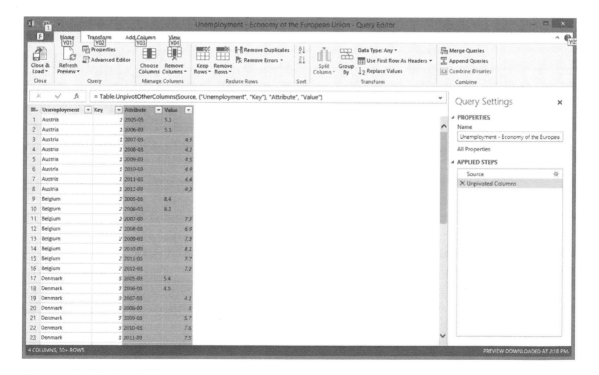

Figure 9-30. *Unpivoted data*

3. Note that the column containing the year is labeled Attribute, which is not descriptive. Right-click the column heading and select Rename to change the name to year. Make sure that only the Attribute column is selected. Then change the data type to date, by selecting the column and clicking the down arrow after Data Type on the top-right side of the ribbon and selecting date. Change the name of the unemployment column to country, change the name of the value column to unemployment, and change the type of the column to decimal number. After changing the type of the unemployment column to decimal number, all data will be right-justified. The data should appear as shown in Figure 9-31. Note that the Applied Steps are shown in the Query Settings pane on the right side of the screen.

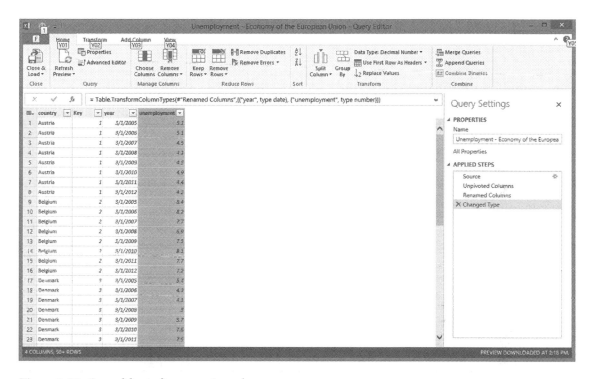

Figure 9-31. *Spreadsheet after renaming columns*

4. Select Close & Load to save to a spreadsheet.

5. At this point, it is important to check the columns for any extraneous data types. For example, if a date column has non-date values, it will not map properly. The best way to check is to sort the columns from lowest to highest and highest to lowest, by pulling down the arrow at the top of each numeric and date column. This process may reveal a row containing only dots, as shown in Figure 9-32. If this is the case, delete this row by highlighting the row, right-clicking, and selecting delete and table rows.

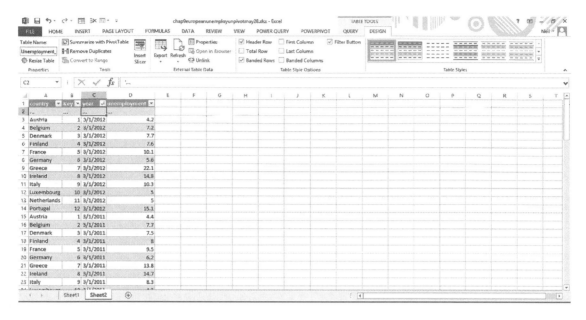

***Figure 9-32.** Extraneous row containing ellipses at top*

6. Check the formatting on the year column by selecting the column and right-clicking, making sure that a date format is selected, as shown in Figure 9-33.

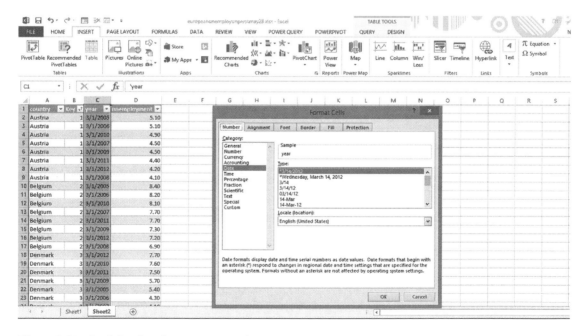

***Figure 9-33.** Applying date format to year column*

7. Also, check the format for the unemployment column, making sure that it has a number format with two places to the right of the decimal point, as shown in Figure 9-34.

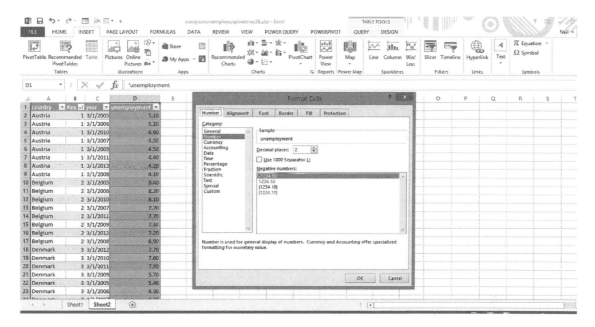

Figure 9-34. *Applying number format to unemployment column*

8. Then select the Insert tab and click Map and Launch Power Map.

9. Click the Refresh Data icon on the ribbon. This is important for applying the formatting changes.

10. Confirm that country is the geographic field by clicking Next, as shown in Figure 9-35.

Figure 9-35. *Defining geographic field*

11. Click Map Labels on the ribbon, then click the unemployment field to select the metric to be plotted and drag the legend box to the left, as shown in Figure 9-36.

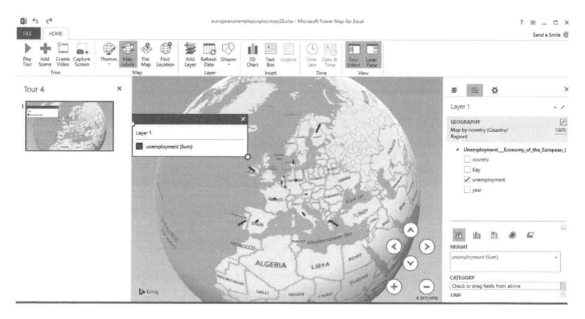

Figure 9-36. *Selecting unemployment metric*

12. Change the aggregation of the unemployment field to no aggregation by clicking the arrow after unemployment in the Height window and selecting No Aggregation, as shown in Figure 9-37.

Figure 9-37. *Changing unemployment aggregation to no aggregation*

13. Right-click year and select Set as Time, as shown in Figure 9-38.

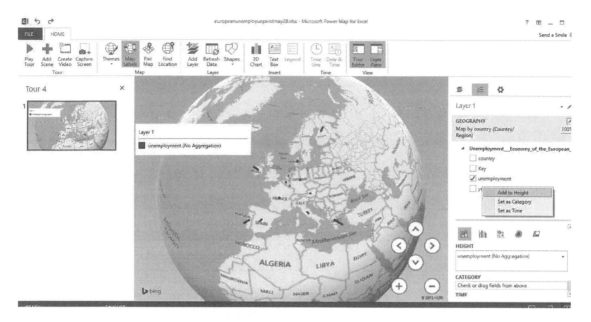

Figure 9-38. *Setting the year as time field*

Notice that a time control appears at the bottom of the map window, and the time appears in a box in the upper left, as shown in Figure 9-39. A time animation can be played by clicking the Play button on the time control at the bottom of the screen.

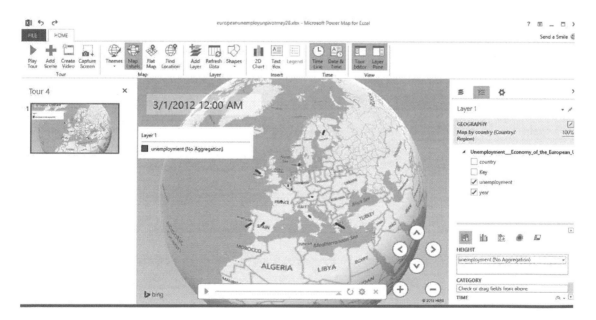

Figure 9-39. *Map set up for time animation*

The speed of play can be adjusted by clicking the gear icon on the upper right and clicking Scene Options to change the scene duration time and effects, as shown in Figure 9-40. The Speed slider at the bottom of the pane can be adjusted to slow down or speed up the transitions.

Figure 9-40. *Setting scene duration*

Summary

This chapter has demonstrated how to load data into Power Query, how to shape the data in the Query Editor, and then how to load it in Power Map to create a visual story about the data. Some of the capabilities of Power Map were demonstrated, such as creating 2D and 3D visualizations, as well as creating animations to show variations over time.

CHAPTER 10

■■■

Statistical Calculations

Excel provides a variety of built-in tools for performing statistical analysis. This chapter highlights some of those tools, including basic charting and the Excel Analysis ToolPak. The difference between descriptive and inferential statistics is discussed, and Excel statistical functions are introduced.

Recommended Analytical Tools in 2013

Excel 2013 tries to anticipate your needs by recommending conditional formatting, charts, tools, totals, and Pivot Tables. When data is highlighted, or when Ctrl+Q is pressed, with any cell in the data range selected, a pop-up window with various formatting options is displayed, as shown in Figure 10-1. Moving the cursor over the conditional formatting options will show a preview of that conditional formatting on the data.

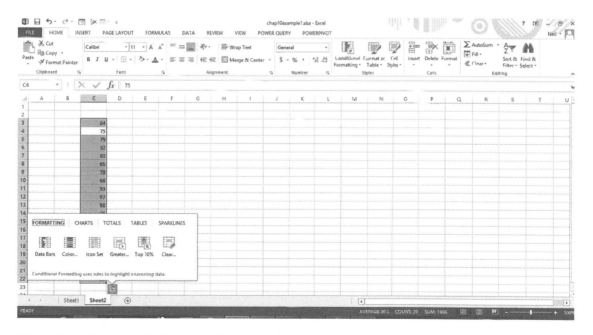

Figure 10-1. *Recommended format and analytics options*

Clicking Totals in the pop-up window will cause the Totals menu to be displayed, which is shown in Figure 10-2.

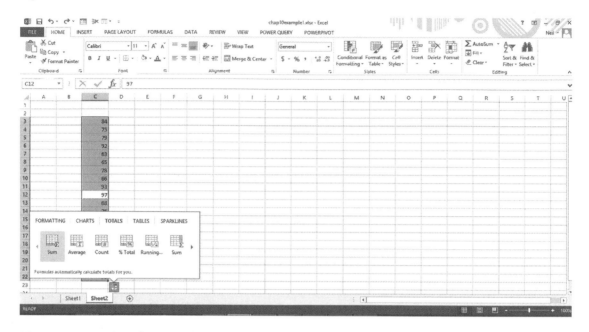

Figure 10-2. *Totals and statistical options*

Scrolling right to highlight % Total will produce the results shown in Figure 10-3, in which the percent of the total is shown to the right of each item.

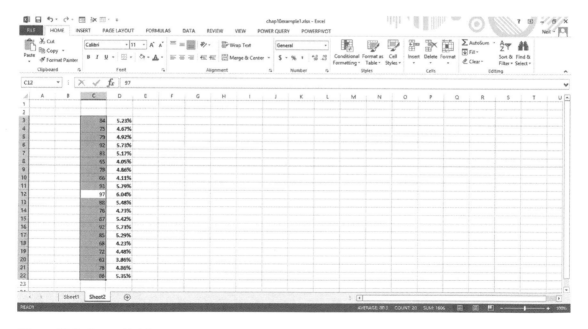

Figure 10-3. *Percent totals*

Customizing the Status Bar

Notice that the status bar at the bottom of the Excel window shows statistics related to the highlighted data, such as the average, count, and sum. You can customize the values shown by right-clicking the status bar and selecting the items you want displayed, as shown in Figure 10-4.

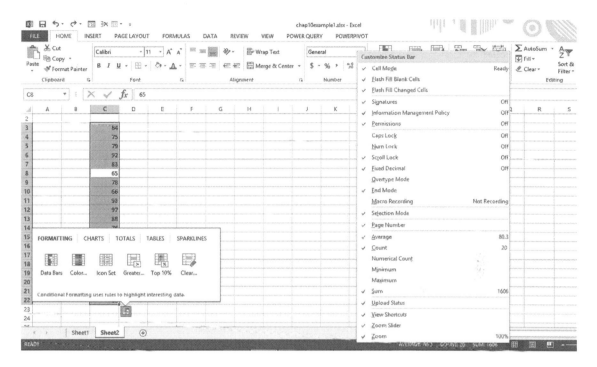

Figure 10-4. *Customize Status Bar menu*

If Minimum and Maximum, for example, are selected on the Customize Status Bar menu, those values will be added to the status bar, as shown in Figure 10-5.

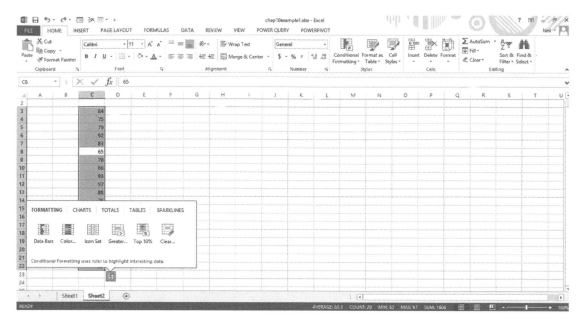

Figure 10-5. *Status bar with Min and Max added*

Inferential Statistics

Sampling involves examining a small portion of a large population in order to draw conclusions about the entire population. This is called inferential statistics. For a sample to be representative of the larger population, the members of the sample must be selected randomly, meaning that every member of the population has the same chance of being included as any other member. The objective is to draw reliable conclusions about the population from the sample. Determining the sample size is critical. The margin of error for a sample is calculated as one divided by the square root of the sample size. Thus, as the sample size increases, the margin of error decreases.

Generally, a sample is used because it is not economically feasible to survey an entire population. One of the promises of big data is that if the data is available, an entire population can be processed for more accurate results.

Review of Descriptive Statistics

Descriptive statistics summarize data with a few key calculated values. Figure 10-6 shows a normal distribution or, bell, curve. The frequency with which any value occurs is represented by the height of the curve. For example, if a coin is tossed ten times over multiple trials, the average number of heads will be five. This is the result that will occur most frequently and is represented by the highest point of the curve. The next most common occurrence will be six heads and four tails or six tails and four heads. Rarely would there be nine heads and one tail.

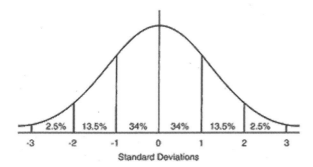

Figure 10-6. Bell curve

Calculating Descriptive Statistics

The most common calculated statistical values are mean, median, and mode.

> The mean, the average or arithmetic mean, is computed by adding all the values and dividing by the number of values.

> The middle value is called the median—the data point at which 50% of the values fall above it and 50% of the values fall below it.

> The most frequent value is called the mode. In a bell curve, the median, mode, and mean are equal.

Measures of Dispersion

Many distributions don't fit neatly into a bell curve, however, so we need measures of dispersion. The variance measures how far a set of numbers is spread out. A small variance indicates that the data points tend to be very close to the mean and, hence, to each other, while a high variance indicates that the data points are very spread out around the mean and from each other.

One measure of dispersion is the standard deviation, which is calculated by computing the deviation of each value from the arithmetic mean and squaring them. The arithmetic mean of these squared values is calculated, and the square root taken to calculate the standard deviation is represented by the Greek letter sigma.

The 68-95-99 rule is used to remember what percentage of values fall within a range around the mean of a normal distribution. In other words, 68.27% of the values are within the range of plus or minus one standard deviation; 95.45% of the values are in a range of plus or minus two standard deviations; and 99.73% of the values are within a range of plus or minus three standard deviations. This is sometimes called the Three Sigma Rule of Thumb. Remember that this rule only applies to a normal distribution. Notice the percentages shown in the illustration in Figure 10-6 that correspond to this rule.

For example, in an analysis of home values, if all home sales fall within a fairly narrow range, such as $400,000 to $600,000, there would be a relatively small variance and standard deviation. However, if a couple of high-end homes sell for more than $1,000,000, there would be a larger variance and standard deviation. That is why the graphical approaches described in the remainder of this chapter are useful for showing relationships among values.

Excel Statistical Functions

Excel provides numerous functions to calculate statistical values. Here are a few of the more common ones.

Average(range): Calculates the arithmetic mean of a range of data or a list of discrete values. It ignores empty cells or cells containing text.

Averagea(range): Same as average, except that it assigns a value of zero to cells containing text.

Averageif(range, condition): Returns an arithmetic mean based on a conditional statement enclosed in quotes. It does not include empty cells or cells containing text in calculations.

Averageifs(range,condition1,condition2): Returns an arithmetic mean based on multiple conditional statements. It does not include empty cells or cells containing text in calculations.

Median(range): Calculates the media or middle value.

Mode(range): Calculates the most frequent value, excluding empty cells and cells containing text not counted.

Charting Data

Excel provides several ways of viewing data graphically. It is important to select the best graphical tool to accurately portray the data, as described in the list below.

- Column and bar charts plot a category variable on one axis and a numeric variable on the other.

- An XY scatter chart shows the relationship between two numeric values.

- Frequency distributions deal with one variable only—it shows how many instances there are of each value. It groups individual measurements into classes or bins. In its most common form, the variable's values are on the horizontal, or x, axis and the frequency of instances on the vertical, or y, axis

- A histogram is a graphical representation of the distribution of numerical data.

Excel Analysis ToolPak

This section will cover how to use the Excel Analysis ToolPak, which is included with Excel. The Analysis ToolPak can be used to perform sophisticated statistical calculations that would be very time-consuming to program in by hand.

Enabling the Excel Analysis ToolPak

Before use, it must be activated.

To enable the Excel Analysis ToolPak, follow these steps:

1. Click the File tab to see the Backstage View.

2. Click Options at the bottom of the left pane.

3.   Select Add-Ins on the left pane.

4.   At the bottom of the window, select Excel Add-Ins and click Go, as shown in
     Figure 10-7.

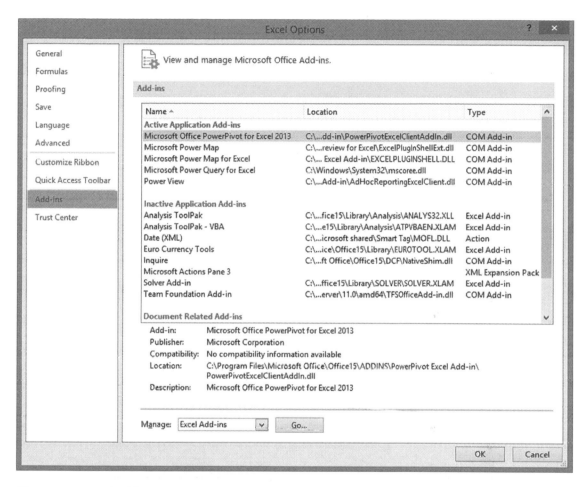

Figure 10-7. *Excel Add-Ins screen*

5.   Select Analysis TookPak, as shown in Figure 10-8, and click OK.

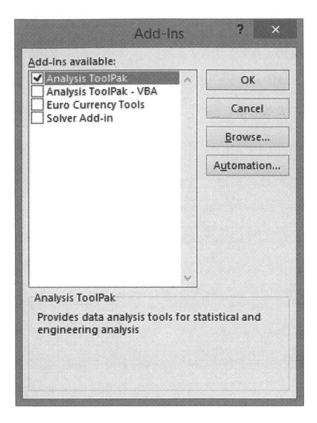

Figure 10-8. *Add-Ins pop-up*

After activation, the Analysis ToolPak can now be accessed by clicking Data Analysis on the right side of the Data tab in Excel.

A Simple Example

The following example will show how to use the Excel Analysis ToolPak to analyze some sample test scores.

EXERCISE 10-1. USING THE ANALYSIS TOOLPAK

Follow these steps to analyze the test score:

1. Click Data Analysis on the right side of the Data tab. When the Data Analysis windows appears, select Descriptive Statistics, as shown in Figure 10-9.

Figure 10-9. *Data Analysis tools*

2. Click OK. In the Descriptive Statistics dialog box, specify the input range and the output range and select summary statistics, as shown in Figure 10-10, and click OK.

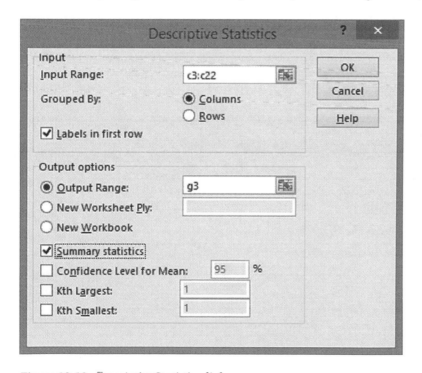

Figure 10-10. *Descriptive Statistics dialog*

The results are shown in Figure 10-11.

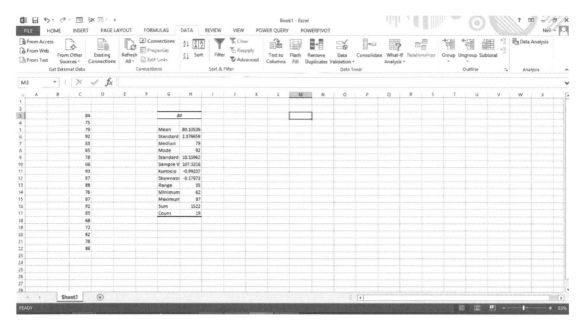

Figure 10-11. *Descriptive Statistics output*

3.   To plot a histogram using the Data Analysis ToolPak, go to the Data tab and click Data Analytics. Select Histogram, as shown in Figure 10-12.

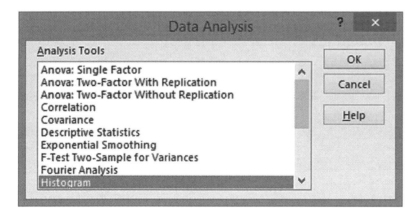

Figure 10-12. *Selecting Histogram from the Data Analysis dialog*

4.   Define the range and select chart output, as shown in Figure 10-13, and click OK.

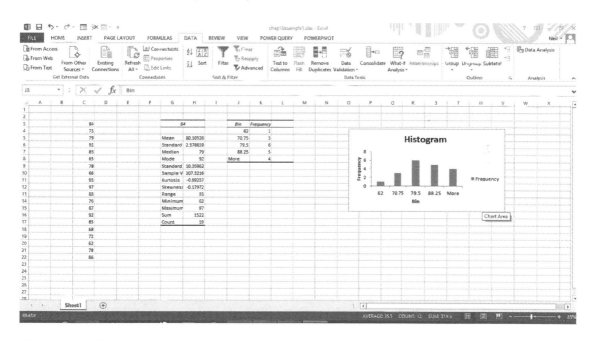

Figure 10-13. *Histogram dialog*

The results are shown in Figure 10-14. This operation sets up bins, or categories, for classifying the data, which are used for plotting the histogram.

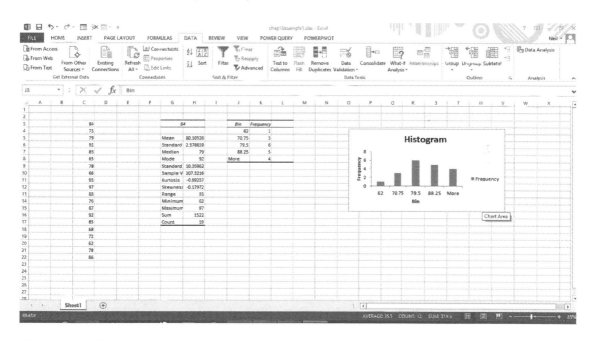

Figure 10-14. *Histogram plot*

Other Analysis ToolPak Functions

The Analysis ToolPak includes other functions. Some of the most useful ones are listed following:

- The Anova tools provide different types of variance analysis. They test the randomness of the selection of two samples.

- The correlation coefficient is a value between -1 and +1 that measures how strongly two variables are related to each other. A +1 indicates a perfect positive correlation, meaning that the two variables move together. A -1 indicates a perfect negative correlation, meaning that the two variables move in opposition to each other. A positive correlation does not prove cause and effect. The Excel CORREL function can also be used to calculate correlation.

- Covariance is a measure of how much two random variables change together.

- Exponential smoothing is like a moving average used to forecast the next value in a time series.

Using a Pivot Table to Create a Histogram

A Pivot Table can also be used to create a more customized histogram.

EXERCISE 10-2. A CUSTOMIZED TEST SCORE HISTOGRAM EXAMPLE

Create a histogram that shows test score distributions by following these steps:

1. Highlight the data to be plotted. Select the Insert tab and click PivotTable.

2. Confirm the range and put the Pivot Table in the same worksheet with the location of F3, as shown in Figure 10-15.

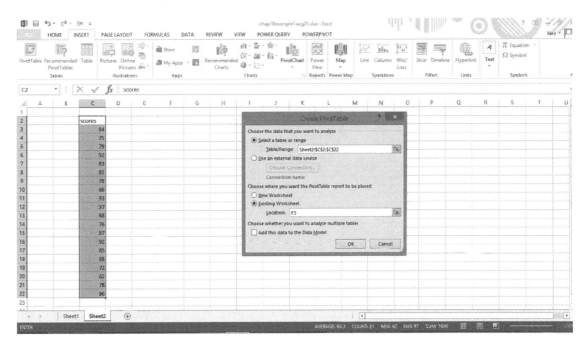

Figure 10-15. *Create PivotTable dialog*

3. Drag scores to the Rows box, as shown in Figure 10-16.

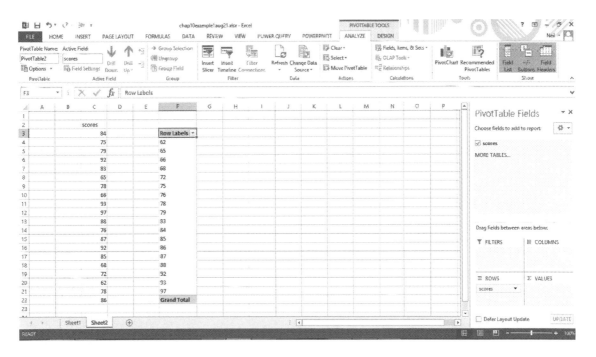

Figure 10-16. *Test scores as rows*

4. Right-click the PivotTable column and select Group, as shown in Figure 10-17.

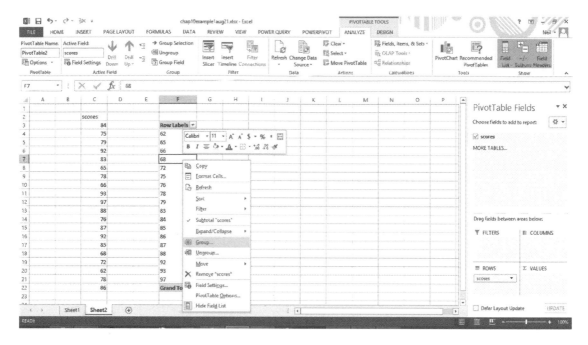

Figure 10-17. Selecting Group from the context menu

5. By default, the Grouping dialog box sets the lower range to the lowest score and the upper range to the highest score, with a default interval of 10, as shown in Figure 10-18. Click OK.

Figure 10-18. Grouping dialog

6. Drag the scores to the Value box. The result indicating the frequency for each grouping category is shown in Figure 10-19. Notice that the categories are approximately what the grading categories would be: 92 to 100 would be an A, 82 to 91 would be a B, etc.

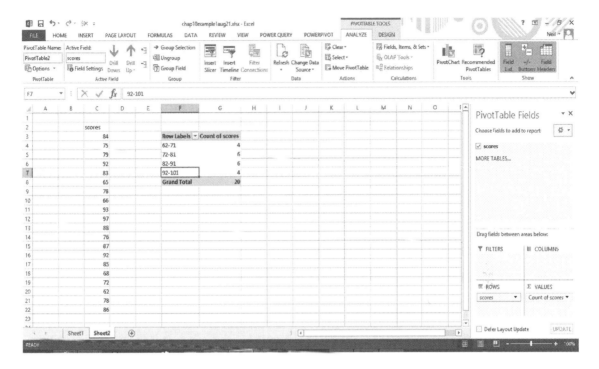

Figure 10-19. *Grouping categories*

7. To plot a histogram, click the Insert tab and select Column Chart, 2D Column. The result, which plots the frequency for each category, is shown in Figure 10-20.

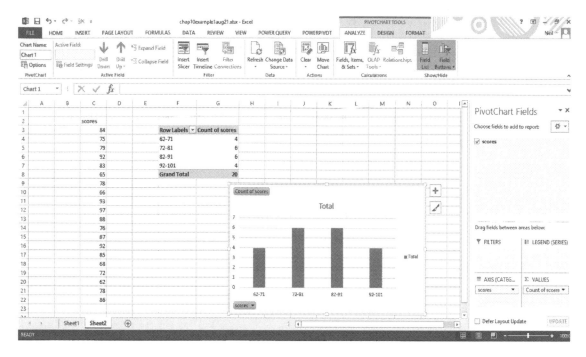

Figure 10-20. *Histogram*

8. The chart can be tweaked by clicking a column and pressing Ctrl+1 to open the Format Data Series pane on the right side of the screen. Adjust the Gap Width slider to zero to remove the space between columns.

9. The title can be modified by clicking the title, which now says Total, and changing it to "Frequency Distribution of Test Scores," as shown in Figure 10-21.

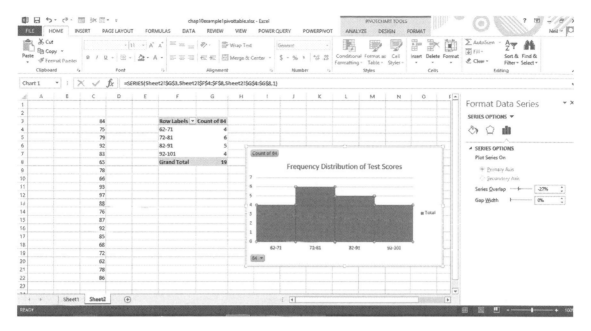

Figure 10-21. *Histogram with title*

Scatter Chart

It is possible to see the visual relationship between two variables by plotting a scatter chart and then allowing the program to calculate the R-squared value. R-squared is a statistical measure of how close the data are to the fitted regression line—the best-fitting straight line through the points. It is also known as the coefficient of determination. R-squared values range from 0 to 100. An R-squared value of 100 means that all movements of one value are completely explained by movements of the other variable. X is the independent variable, and y is the dependent variable.

EXERCISE 10-3. GRADE-ABSENCE RELATIONSHIP SCATTER CHART EXAMPLE

This example explores whether there is a relationship between class absences and numeric grades, with 1 being the lowest grade and 4 the highest. The grade data is shown in Figure 10-22.

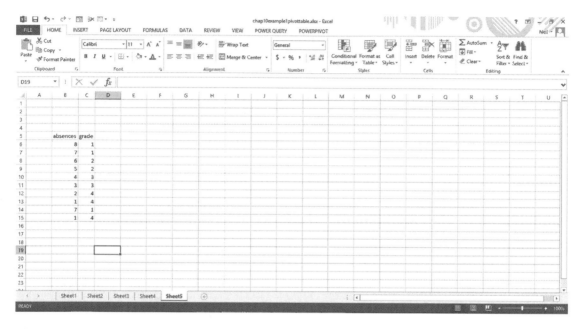

Figure 10-22. *Grade and absence data*

Follow these steps:

1. Highlight the data, click the Insert tab, and select Scatter (X, Y), as shown in Figure 10-23.

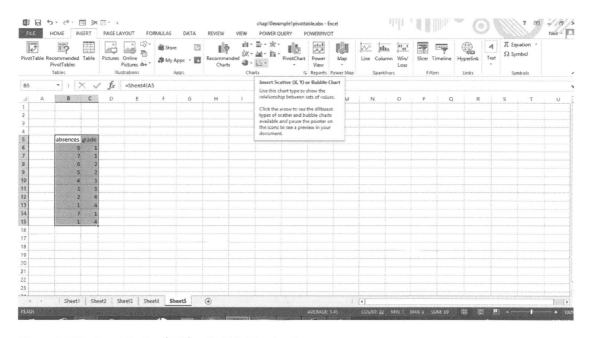

Figure 10-23. *Insert Scatter (X, Y) or Bubble Chart option*

2. Select the Scatter option, as shown in Figure 10-24.

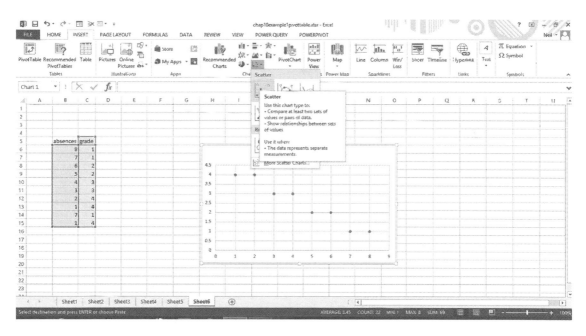

Figure 10-24. *Select Scatter option*

3. Click the + sign at the upper right of the chart and select Axis Titles, as shown in Figure 10-25.

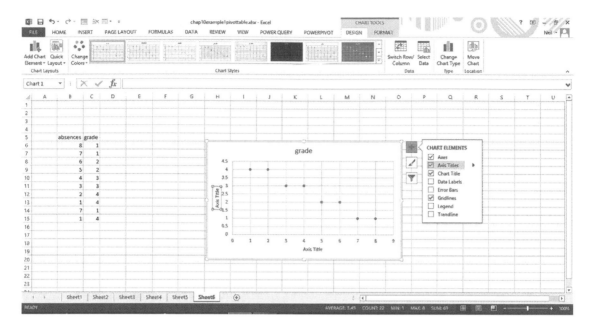

Figure 10-25. *Select Axis Titles*

4. Click the Axis Title on the horizontal or x axis and change it to Absences. Change the label on the vertical, or y, axis to Grades and change the chart title to "Relationship between Grade and Absences," as shown in Figure 10-26.

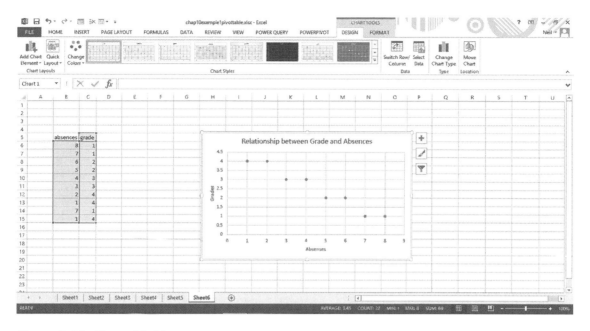

Figure 10-26. *Chart with title*

5. Right-click the plot area and select Add Trendline…, as shown in Figure 10-27.

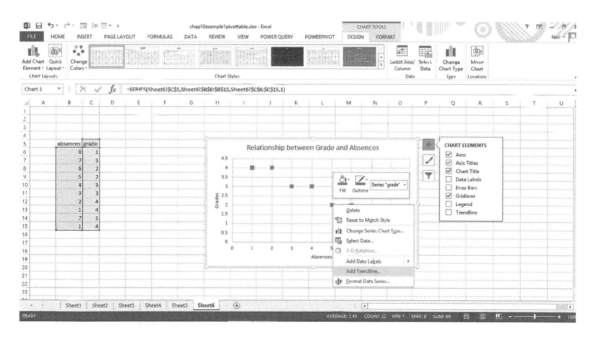

Figure 10-27. *Select Add Trendline…*

6. In the Format Trendline pane on the right, scroll down and select Display Equation on Chart and Display R squared value on chart, as shown in Figure 10-28. The formula for the line, including the slope and y intercept, is shown. Note that the R-squared value of 0.9603 (shown in decimal form) indicates a high correlation. This is an inverse relationship, which means the more absences, the lower the grade.

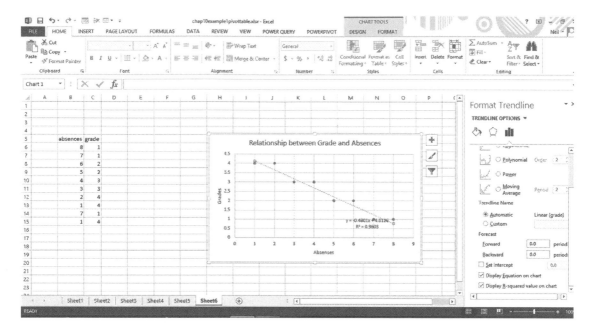

Figure 10-28. *Chart showing the formula and R-squared value*

Summary

This chapter has only begun to scratch the surface of the ability of Excel to calculate statistical values by using the Excel Analysis ToolPak. It has shown how to create visual displays of data, using the built-in charting tools. It has shown how to determine whether there is a relationship between two values. An entire book could be written on these topics.

CHAPTER 11

■ ■ ■

HDInsight

Chapter 1 described Hadoop as an open source distributed file system that allows processing of vast amounts of data. Microsoft's implementation of Hadoop on its Azure cloud platform is called HDInsight, which is designed to handle large amounts of data in the cloud. HDInsight uses Azure blob storage for storing the data, to make Hadoop available as a service in the cloud. Azure is useful for storing large datasets in the cloud in a cost-effective manner. Microsoft only charges for resources actually used.

Apache Hive supports analysis of large datasets stored in Hadoop. Hive is a data warehouse infrastructure built on top of Hadoop for providing data summarization, query, and analysis. Originally developed by Facebook, it is now an open source Apache project.

This chapter explores the easiest way to export data for analysis from Azure HDInsight into Excel.

Getting a Free Azure Account

Earlier chapters covered how to use the Azure Data Marketplace, which is essentially free for certain databases. The example in this chapter requires an Azure account. A 30-day trial account can be obtained by going to https://azure.microsoft.com/en-us/pricing/free-trial/.

The screen shown in Figure 11-1 will appear.

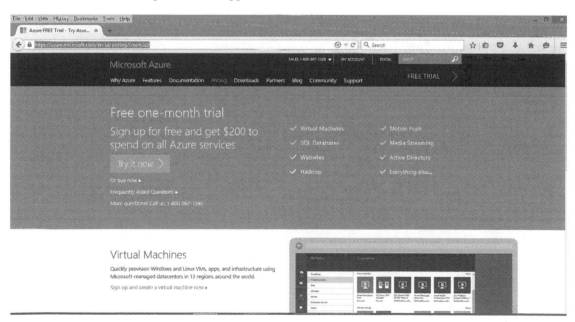

Figure 11-1. Azure free trial screen as of July 2015

225

Click Try It now, and you will be prompted to enter your information to set up a free one-month trial.

Importing Hadoop Files into Power Query

This example shows how to run a Hive query on a large dataset, using an HDInsight on Windows Azure Blob Storage. It then demonstrates how to use Power Query to import the data into Excel, so that it can be analyzed using Pivot Tables and Power Map.

Creating an Azure Storage Account

To do this tutorial, you need the Windows Azure account just created.

1. Sign in to the Azure portal

    ```
    https://manage.windowsazure.com
    ```

    The screen shown in Figure 11-2 will appear. Log in with your Azure credentials.

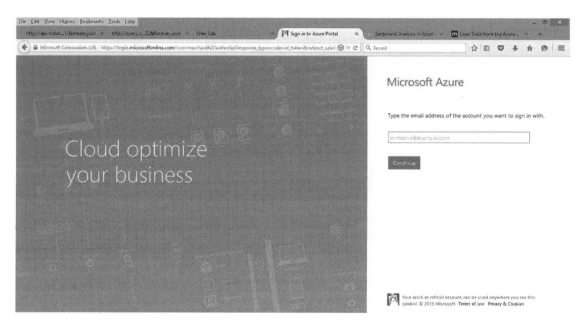

Figure 11-2. *Microsoft Azure portal*

2. After logging in, click +NEW at the lower left-hand corner of the Azure portal screen, as shown in Figure 11-3.

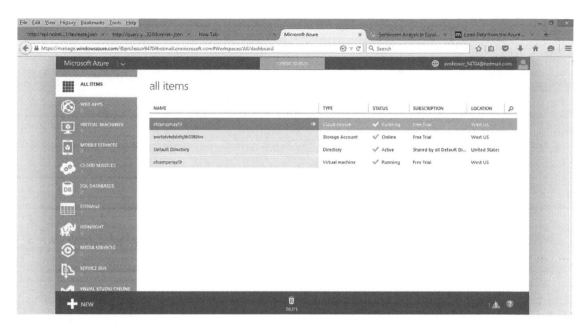

Figure 11-3. Azure portal screen

3. Select Data Services ➤ Storage and Quick Create, as shown in Figure 11-4. Enter a unique name for the URL. This example will use testhive. Select a location closest to where you are.

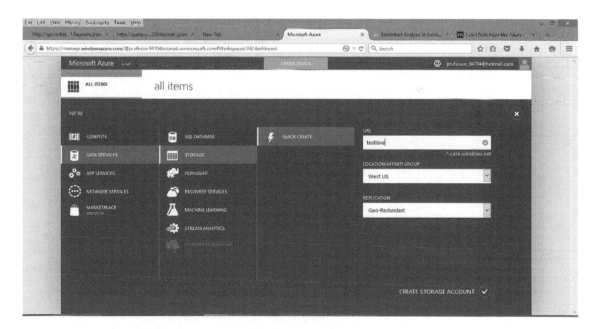

Figure 11-4. Setting up a storage account in Azure

4. Click Create Storage Account in the lower right and wait for the account to be created. The resulting screen will appear, as shown in Figure 11-5.

Figure 11-5. *New storage account*

5. Highlight the new account and click Manage Access Keys at the bottom of the screen. The Manage Access Keys pop-up will appear, as shown in Figure 11-6. Notice the primary and secondary access keys. Clicking the icon to the right of the key will copy it to the clipboard. Click the check mark at the bottom right of the screen, to close the window.

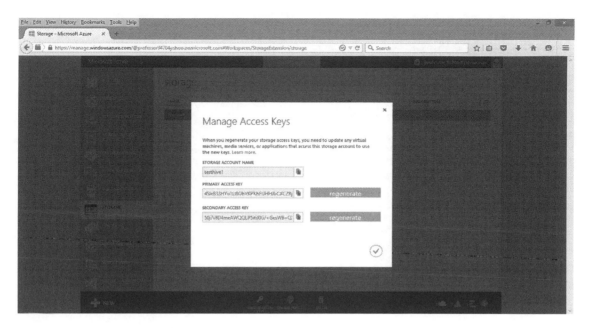

Figure 11-6. *Manage Access Keys*

Provisioning a Hadoop Cluster

To provision a Hadoop Cluster, follow these steps:

1. Click +NEW in the lower left corner of the screen.

2. Select Data Services ➤ HDInsight ➤ Hadoop and fill in the values on the right side of the screen, as shown in Figure 11-7. Choose a cluster name. Two nodes should be sufficient for this example. Azure sets the default user name to Admin. You will need to create a password of at least ten characters, including at least one capital letter, one number, and one special character, and enter it twice, as prompted. Be sure to remember the password entered.

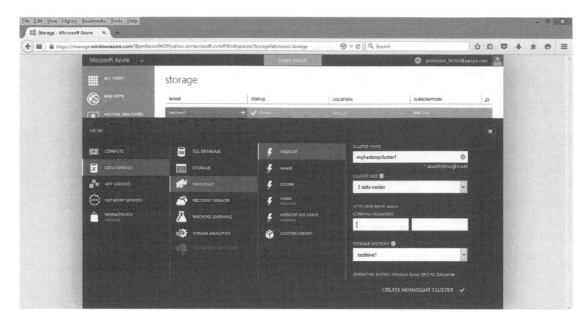

Figure 11-7. *Setting up the HDInsight cluster*

3. Click Create HDInsight Cluster at the bottom lower right of the screen. Then the screen shown in Figure 11-8 will appear after the cluster is created, which may take 20 minutes or more.

Figure 11-8. *Showing new cluster*

4. Click HDInsight from the left pane to see the list of clusters, as shown in Figure 11-9. The cluster that was just created should be shown.

Figure 11-9. *List of HDInsight clusters*

5. Select the cluster that was just created and click Query Console at the bottom of the screen. If requested, enter your admin username and password. The screen shown in Figure 11-10 will appear.

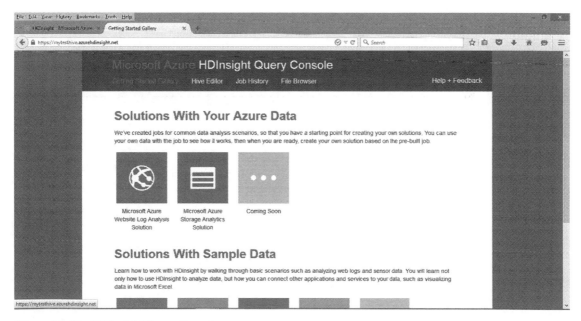

Figure 11-10. *HDInsight Query Console*

6. Scroll down to see Solutions With Sample Data.

7. Click the Hive Editor tab at the top of the screen. In Hive Editor, enter a query name and accept the default SQL as Select * from hivesampletable to select all records as shown in Figure 11-11.

Figure 11-11. *SQL query to select all records*

8. Click Submit.

9. To see the query results, click the query name at the bottom left of the screen, as shown in Figure 11-12.

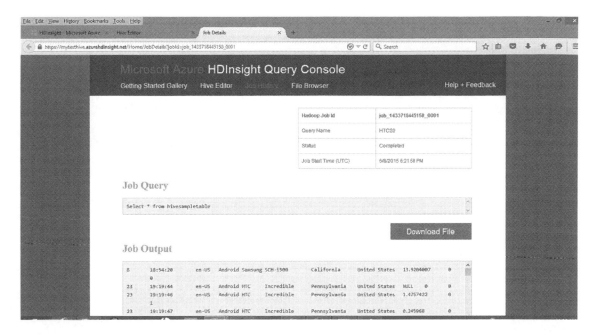

Figure 11-12. *Query results*

> 10. On the HD Query Console screen, click File Browser at the top of the screen. The results are shown in Figure 11-13.

Figure 11-13. *List of clusters*

11. Click the first item in the Name column on the left and then on your cluster name, to get the results shown in Figure 11-14.

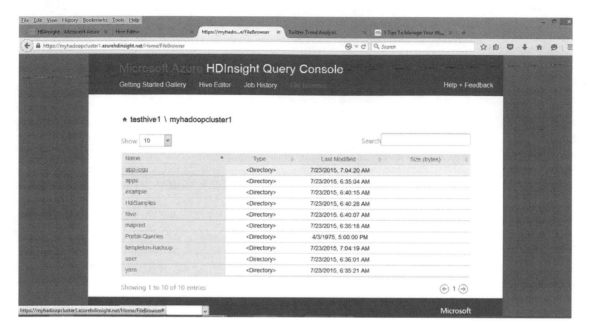

Figure 11-14. *List of files in cluster*

Importing into Excel

There are several ways to import this data into Excel. This section will demonstrate how to download the file to a text file with fixed-length fields.

Follow these steps:

1. Go back to the screen shown in Figure 11-12, by clicking Job History at the top of the screen and then clicking the query name. Then click Download File.

2. The Job Log for the download is shown in Figure 11-15, which reports that 59,793 rows were downloaded. The number you see may differ.

Figure 11-15. *Job Log for downloads*

3. Click the blue box at the bottom of the screen labeled Download File. When prompted for the program to use to open the file, select Notepad. The result will appear in Notepad, as shown in Figure 11-16. This appears to be a log file for web site accesses.

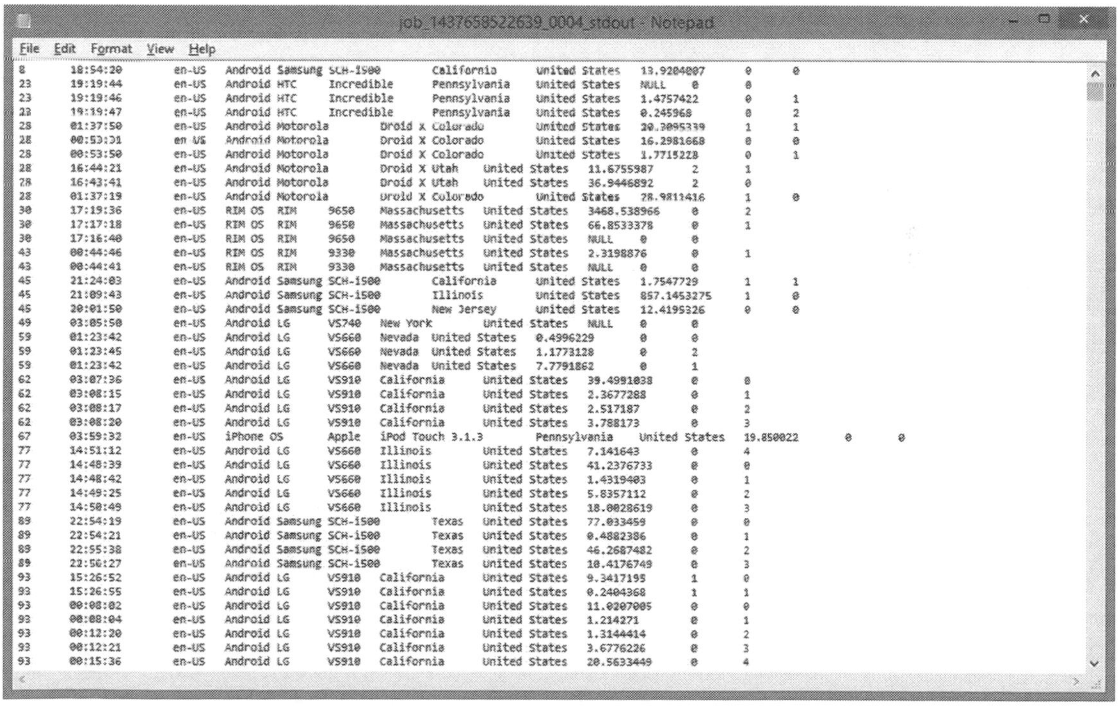

Figure 11-16. *Log file for web site accesses*

4. Do a Save As to save the file to the desktop, to make it easier to access.

5. Open Excel and click the Power Query tab. Select from File and then From Text and Browse to find the downloaded file.

6. The file will be loaded into the Query Editor, as shown in Figure 11-17. Note that Power Query parsed the fixed-length fields to neatly put all the data in separate columns, but there are no descriptive column headings.

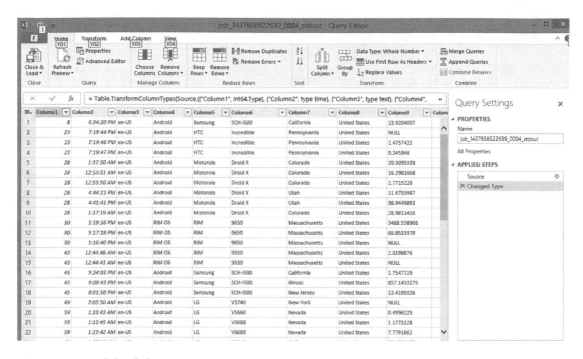

Figure 11-17. *File loaded into Power Query*

7. To rename critical columns, right-click the column heading, select Rename, and enter a new descriptive name, as shown below.

Old Name	New Name
Column2	Datetime
Column4	OS
Column5	Manufacturer
Coluimn6	Model
Column7	State
Column 8	Country
Column10	Accesses

The result is shown in Figure 11-18.

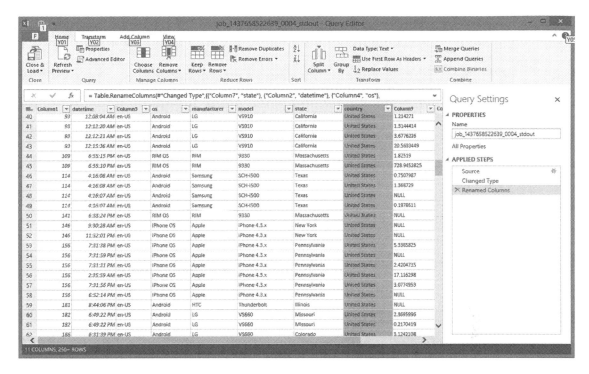

Figure 11-18. *Power Query Editor after columns are renamed*

8. To load the data into a spreadsheet, click Close & Load on the left end of the ribbon and select Close & Load. The data is loaded into a spreadsheet, as shown in Figure 11-19.

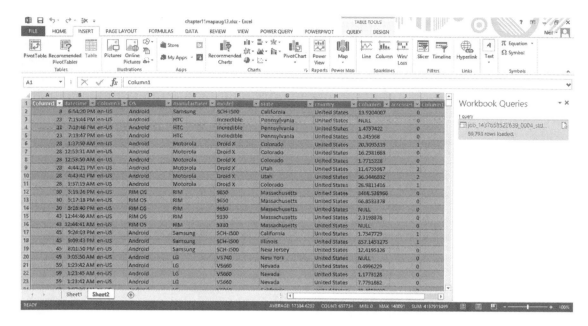

Figure 11-19. *Data loaded into spreadsheet*

Creating a Pivot Table

To create a Pivot Table to analyze accesses by state, manufacturer, and model, follow these steps:

1. Click Insert and Pivot Table. Accept the default of putting it in a new worksheet.

2. Drag state to the Columns box, manufacturer and model to the Rows box, and accesses to the Values box. The result, which shows accesses by manufacturer and model, is shown in Figure 11-20.

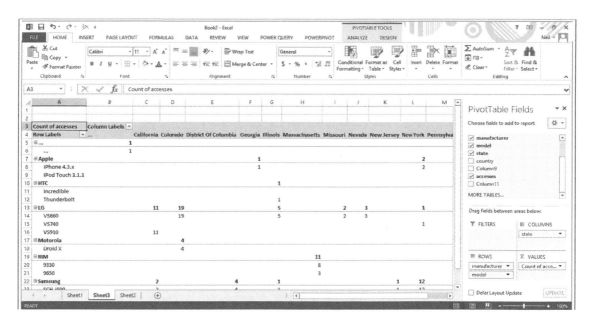

Figure 11-20. *Pivot Table showing accesses by manufactuer and model*

Creating a Map in Power Map

This example shows how to map the data using Power Map. Follow these steps:

1. With the data loaded into the spreadsheet, click the Insert tab and then Map and Launch Power Map

2. Accept the default of country and state as the default geographic fields and click Next, as shown in Figure 11-21.

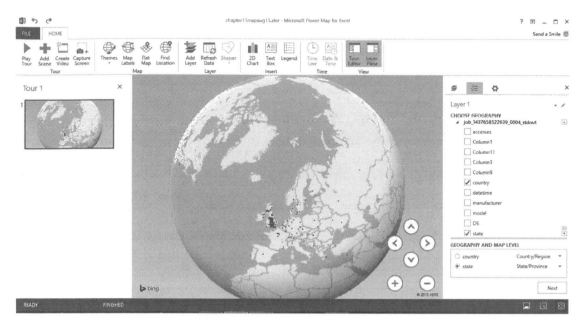

Figure 11-21. *Selecting geographic fields*

3. Click Accesses for height and right-click OS and select Set as Category, as shown in Figure 11-22, which shows the map panned over to the United States.

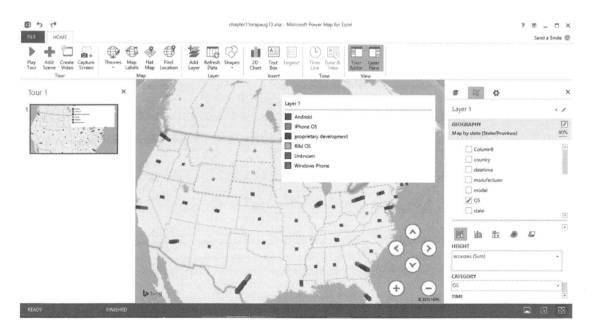

Figure 11-22. *Map showing accesses by OS in the United States*

A similar display for Europe is shown in Figure 11-23.

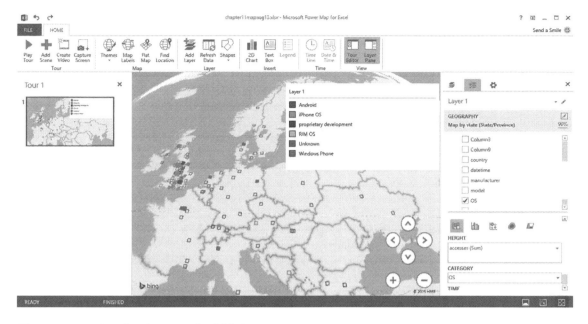

Figure 11-23. *Map showing access by OS in Europe*

If you are finished with the HDInsight cluster you just created, delete it, so that you will not be charged for it.

Summary

This chapter has just scratched the surface of the power of creating and accessing Hadoop clusters in Azure and moving the data into Excel and Power Query for analysis using Pivot Tables and Power Map to provide a graphic display of the data broken out by OS.

Index

■ T, U, V, W, X, Y, Z

Get the eBook for only $5!

Why limit yourself?

Now you can take the weightless companion with you wherever you go and access your content on your PC, phone, tablet, or reader.

Since you've purchased this print book, we're happy to offer you the eBook in all 3 formats for just $5.

Convenient and fully searchable, the PDF version enables you to easily find and copy code—or perform examples by quickly toggling between instructions and applications. The MOBI format is ideal for your Kindle, while the ePUB can be utilized on a variety of mobile devices.

To learn more, go to www.apress.com/companion or contact support@apress.com.